LINKEDIN LEAD GENERATION FOR FINANCIAL ADVISERS

LINKEDIN LEAD GENERATION FOR FINANCIAL ADVISERS

How to Attract More of Your Ideal Clients on LinkedIn – Proven Messaging Scripts and Daily Planner

By Philip Calvert

Copyright© 2020 Philip Calvert

All rights reserved. This book or any portion thereof may not be reproduced or used in any manner whatsoever without the express written permission of the publisher except for the use of brief quotations in a book review or scholarly journal.

First Edition: 2020

ISBN: 979-8-667-89880-1

LinkedIn, the LinkedIn logo, the IN logo and InMail are registered trademarks or trademarks of LinkedIn Corporation and its affiliates in the United States and/or other countries.

SPEAKER, TRAINER & CONSULTANT

Philip Calvert

SOCIAL MEDIA FOR THE NEW ECONOMY

"Genuine conversation around real experiences spark better and deeper conversation. Better conversation, in turn, leads to stronger community and connection."

LinkedIn®

"Stronger community and connection leads to stronger relationships, which in turn, attract more of the clients, referrals and introductions that you really want for your financial advice business."

Philip Calvert

"I used one of your LinkedIn tips straight after your conference presentation yesterday and already have two calls arranged with prospects! People need to see your presentation, follow your advice and then apply it."

Financial Planner, January 2020

Accompanying Marketing and Lead Generation Resources

Free LinkedIn Health Check for Financial Advisers:
https://linkedinforadvisers.scoreapp.com

Free Marketing Health Check for Financial Advisers:
https://financialadvisermarketing.scoreapp.com

Marketing and Lead Generation Community for Financial Planners, IFAs and Professional Financial Advisers
https://www.financialadvice.marketing

Book: Marketing for Financial Advice Professionals - Proven Tips and Techniques to Attract More of your Dream Clients in the Digital Age
https://bit.ly/AdviserMarketing

Book Philip to Train your Team or Speak at your Event:
www.philipcalvert.com

Contents

PART ONE 11

Accompanying Marketing and Lead Generation Resources

Introduction

How much business from LinkedIn are you missing out on?

Learn to love LinkedIn - Forty-nine reasons for Financial Advisers to master LinkedIn

Twenty-one 'must do' action points for winning with LinkedIn and attracting more of the clients and connections you really want

Proven LinkedIn Messaging and Connection Scripts

Networking like a Pro: Networking questions that build relationships online and offline

PART TWO 89

Planning your LinkedIn activity

Recommended actions

Getting started – the Five Golden areas of daily activity

Part 1

Part 2

Part 3

Part 4

Part 5

Optional additional activity

A word about Compliance

Your Daily Planner and Journal 137

About the Author

Disclaimer and Terms of Use

PART ONE

Introduction

I've been using LinkedIn since the beginning. And before that I used a website called Ecademy.com – believed to be the world's first B2B social networking site.

Ecademy started in 1998 and for many years did much the same as LinkedIn does now, so they were way ahead of their time.

In fact, I created the world's first online networking group for financial advisers on the Ecademy platform. Just as you can create groups on LinkedIn based round common interests, you could do the same on Ecademy.

I invited IFAs and advisers to join the group, where they could network, share best practice, exchange ideas, get answers to technical questions and provide help and support to one another. It quickly became popular amongst advisers, with many telling me that it was an invaluable industry platform.

Unfortunately, in many ways Ecademy became a victim of its own success, and when LinkedIn and others came along with far bigger budgets for development and growth, Ecademy sadly disappeared, as did our group.

However, as LinkedIn began to grow, I recreated our community for financial advisers (LifeTalk) on that platform, and in recent years extended it to a Facebook group. Even today, there is not a single question about how to be a successful financial adviser or run a profitable IFA business that cannot be answered in our groups.

Take a look:

LifeTalk on LinkedIn: www.linkedin.com/groups/37543

LifeTalk on Facebook: www.facebook.com/groups/AdviserLifeTalk

I also run a separate marketing related group for IFAs, Financial Planners and Advisers at https://www.financialadvice.marketing

But many of the people I met on Ecademy are active today on LinkedIn and happily reminisce about those early days of online social networking.

I first discovered Ecademy in 2002 as a recently new entrant to the world of self-employment. To discover a website where I could 'meet' people online and refer them and their services to others without the need to exchange business cards in the flesh was a revelation.

That is not to suggest that face to face networking is not important. In fact, it is more important than ever. But what many people forget (or perhaps do not fully appreciate) is that social networking sites are NOT a shortcut for building robust business relationships.

The most successful users of LinkedIn realise and know that the site is a **conduit for discovery and for facilitating conversations** that can later build to business. At its heart, LinkedIn is a search engine – the people search engine.

Let's just repeat that because it is extremely important:

*The most successful users of LinkedIn realise and know that the site is a **conduit for discovery and for facilitating conversations** that can later build to business.*

Many financial advisers believe that just having a profile on LinkedIn will be sufficient, and that all the norms of fostering trust, credibility and relationships can be neatly side-tracked. Unfortunately, that is not the case. Successful networking online has nothing to do with the technology – it's about technique.

In this guide I have tried to get to the heart of what LinkedIn is all about and how IFAs, financial planners, wealth managers and professional financial advisers can use it to attract more of the clients and connections that they really want and care about.

Hopefully you will find it to be an easy read, with proven tips, tricks, strategies and scripts that you can take away and implement in your business straight away.

Later in the book you will find a planner which you can use to plot your progress. Follow its steps and watch those relationships develop and flourish.

Note

From time to time LinkedIn tweaks its algorithm, which in turn changes the emphasis on what it believes is important to gain traction on the site. However, I regularly update this book so that you will always have the most up to date information available.

How much business from LinkedIn are you missing out on?

Before we go any further, it's really important that we run a quick audit on how well you are currently using LinkedIn.

Like a lot of things in life, in order to get to where we want to be, we first need to know where we are starting from.

Please go to the link below, where you will find my **LinkedIn Health Check** tool. It is a series of short questions designed to assess what features of LinkedIn you are using and how well you are leveraging the platform overall.

The questions are divided into sections covering your profile, how you engage with people on the site, content and posts and LinkedIn features.

Take the test, get your score and then come back here to record your LinkedIn Health Check score:

https://linkedinforadvisers.scoreapp.com

My total score is: …………%

How do you feel about your score now that you have taken the test?

Don't worry if it is a little lower than you were expecting, we've got you covered. This book reveals everything you need to do to become a LinkedIn superstar and attract more of the clients and connections that you really want as a financial advice professional.

Three months after reading this book (even a month will do), take the test again and see how much you have improved.

The simple truth is that unless your financial advice business only targets clients who are aged eighty or over, you are missing out on high quality leads and enquiries from LinkedIn. Yes, many of those same prospects are also on Facebook, but the overwhelming majority of financial advisers feel more comfortable using LinkedIn for all sorts of reasons we are all too familiar with.

Fact: If you are on LinkedIn, you are marketing yourself – whether you like it or not. And if you are not already receiving enquiries out of the blue from your target clients on LinkedIn, then arguably you are not marketing yourself well enough and you are literally leaking leads.

This book and planner will plug those leaks and give you a proven methodology to turn LinkedIn into a true marketing asset of your business.

Learn to Love LinkedIn: Forty-Nine Reasons for Financial Advisers to Master LinkedIn

Whilst every internet marketer shouts about the awesome power of Facebook to drive traffic, attract leads and to win new clients and customers, sitting quietly behind the scenes is another lead generating monster…

And this is important to understand, because since I first started our group for financial advisers on Ecademy, the number one question asked by advisers in our groups over the years has consistently been, *"What's the best way to generate new leads?"*

When financial advisers join our Facebook group, we always ask them what their biggest issue is as an IFA, financial planner etc. The most common answer is lead generation.

The truth is most people look at LinkedIn and wonder what the fuss is all about.

Whenever I speak at a conference or event, I always ask the audience to let me know if they are on LinkedIn – and almost everyone puts up their hand.

But when I then ask who knows *why* they are on LinkedIn, hardly anyone puts up their hand!

So, why are we all on LinkedIn if we don't know what we're doing there?

It's simple. Herd mentality has a lot to do with it.

And probably someone once told you that you *need* to be on LinkedIn.

Everyone else is on there, so I better be on there too...

True, you might well be looking for a job, in which case you have an obvious reason to be on LinkedIn.

And there is the clue – if you are going to get the best out of the platform, you need to have a clear reason for being there.

There could be many reasons why you are on LinkedIn. Here are forty-nine to get you started:

1. To look for a new job
2. To learn about companies where you might want to work
3. To post job opportunities
4. To build a new career
5. To build your personal brand
6. To build trust and reputation
7. To establish credibility
8. To help you appear in Google search results
9. To attract new clients and customers
10. To share your knowledge and expertise with others
11. To network with fellow professionals and those outside your immediate network
12. To re-connect with friends from school or college

13. To stay up to date on what is happening within your network
14. To follow thought leaders
15. To position yourself as an expert or thought leader
16. To follow certain companies and organisations
17. To increase the visibility of your communications
18. To attract leads
19. To drive traffic to your website
20. To build your newsletter list
21. To reach out to, and engage with influencers in your market
22. To sell your products and services
23. To find distributors, providers and suppliers
24. To find joint venture partners
25. To build community around your brand
26. To share announcements from your company
27. To help employees to become brand ambassadors
28. To help your company to differentiate itself from your competition
29. To join special interest groups
30. To get answers and solutions to problems
31. To teach staff and colleagues how to use social media more effectively in business
32. To help your CEO and leadership team to become 'social leaders'
33. To promote your seminars and events
34. To share your seminar or sales PowerPoint presentations
35. To meet journalists and increase media mentions
36. To highlight your skills
37. To highlight your work or business achievements

38. To highlight awards that you have won
39. To highlight your books and publications
40. To highlight your volunteer experience
41. To find a mentor
42. To make yourself available as a mentor
43. To publish testimonials
44. To get endorsements for your skills
45. To connect with people who have similar interests
46. To see who is following your updates or who has viewed your profile
47. To discover how your salary compares with others with the same expertise
48. To learn new skills
49. To find service providers for a project (not available globally)
50. And much more...!

The key thing is not to be a passive bystander on LinkedIn.

If you are going to have a presence there, then you will get so much more out of it if you have a clearly defined reason and a plan for how you are going to use it.

If you don't, you will end up being one of those people who says:

"I don't get LinkedIn"

or

"I'm fed up with recruiters wanting to connect with me"

or

"There are too many spammers".

In other words, you cannot see the wood for the trees.

At the end of the day, LinkedIn is a piece of software, and like all software that you use in your financial advice business such as your CRM, back office system, cashflow modelling tool, mortgage sourcing, wrap platform etc., unless you take time to learn how to use it, you will most likely never really benefit from it to the full extent that you could.

Still need convincing that LinkedIn works for IFAs and Financial Planners?

Meet Tony – a Chartered Financial Planner in the west of England.

I was talking to Tony last week and we were discussing how he attracts new clients.

"Twenty percent from referrals, twenty percent from ad hoc not very strategic general marketing and the rest [60%] from LinkedIn", he said.

From LinkedIn Tony gets approximately one new client enquiry per week, plus three non-client related opportunities each month such as speaking and consulting and radio/podcast interviews.

I came straight out with it,

"What's the secret to your success on LinkedIn Tony?"

He replied,

"It's quite simple really once you know how..."

This is a summary of what Tony said in the form of a simple list. This book puts his list into proper context and gives you a plan to follow:

- Knowing what sort of clients you want (in his case individuals over the age of fifty who are considering their retirement options - in particular, successful entrepreneurs and senior management and executives in corporations)

- Searching for and finding them on LinkedIn – the search tool is your friend

- Observing what these people post or comment about on LinkedIn

- Engaging with their LinkedIn posts, e.g. *"Great post John, thanks for highlighting that"* or *"Thanks for your post Sue – a point well made"* or *"Great read – thanks for sharing that Mike"* etc.

- Really understanding the concerns and worries faced by your target market

- Restricting the connections you make or accept to only people who broadly match your target market(s)

- Commenting generically on other people's posts

- Commenting on other posts that are relevant or of interest to your target market(s)

- Commenting or posting updates on a consistent basis – daily or every other day ideally

- 'Branding' any graphics that you use – i.e. use the same colours and fonts in all graphics

- Following up people who go on to visit your LinkedIn profile without going into sales mode. Just aim to start a friendly conversation and let time take its course

- Make sure that your profile is fully complete

- Treat LinkedIn as an asset of your business – not just as yet another 'shiny new thing'

- Commit to using LinkedIn and believe in it as a marketing tool – that means being proactive and looking for opportunities to engage with people without being salesy

- Not essential but consider having LinkedIn Premium membership. Start with the free version, but as you start to see success, then upgrade as this will accelerate your results

OK, this is the raw material; now let's make some sense of what Tony really means.

Take control of your LinkedIn membership and let's get started...

Top 21 'Must Do' Action Points for Winning with LinkedIn & Attracting More of the Clients and Contacts you Really Want

1. Have A Clear Plan

As said above, sit down and brainstorm WHY you are on LinkedIn and what you want to get out of it.

And the thing about LinkedIn, is that you can do a lot with it, for example it is a:

- Job site
- Networking platform
- Blogging platform
- Social Network
- Marketing tool
- Community building tool
- Live video streaming platform
- Instant messaging service
- Instant voice messaging service
- Instant video messaging service
- Schools and university finding tool for students
- Platform to connect with alumni
- Platform to engage with colleagues and teammates
- Platform to follow thought leaders and influencers
- Platform to express yourself as an expert or thought leader
- Platform to hire local freelancers
- Corporate PR site

- News service
- Lead generation tool
- Learning centre
- Classified ads service
- Salary comparison service
- Sales tool
- Platform to highlight personal causes
- Platform to find a mentor
- Rolodex
- Events platform
- Online learning platform
- Search engine

I could list many more, but each of the above has its own tool within LinkedIn specifically designed for the job, and they are adding new tools and features all of the time.

Given everything you can do on the site, you can see how easy it is to be side-tracked if you do not have a clear plan.

So, on the next page literally write down some goals for your use of LinkedIn. Take a moment right now to come up with up to five goals.

My LinkedIn Goals – i.e. what I want to achieve on the site

1.

2.

3.

4.

5.

Congratulations – you are now one of an elite group of LinkedIn users who has stopped to think *why* they are on the site!

Once you know your goals, write them down and pin them on the wall in front of you.

Once you know *why* you are on LinkedIn, your experience of the platform will be transformed as you will have a renewed sense of purpose and focus.

2. Fully Complete Your Profile

And I mean FULLY complete your profile, because the majority of financial advisers only half-complete this.

Go through every single section and fill it out in detail. Do not skimp on this; time spent on this now will bring big rewards later.

Why spend so much time on completing my profile?

Because LinkedIn rewards profiles that are fully completed by putting them higher in search results. It also gives people a better experience when they visit your page. A half-completed profile always creates a lacklustre impression on the reader.

I have had financial advisers tell me that *immediately* after they fully completed their profile, they started to appear noticeably higher in search results.

Plus, when you fully complete your profile, it increases the likelihood that it will appear in search results when someone Googles your name.

What are the different sections of my LinkedIn profile?

There are more than you think:

- Name
- Name pronunciation tool
- Profile photo
- Header photo
- Contact incl. IM, phone, email & birthday
- Professional headline
- Websites & Twitter
- Open to Recruiters
- Services Provided
- Featured Posts and Images
- Posts, articles & activity summary
- Summary / About
- Current Experience
- Current Experience Details
- Past Experience
- Past Experience Details
- Education
- Education Details
- Volunteer Experiences & Causes
- Skills and endorsements
- Testimonials / Recommendations
- Certifications
- Courses

- Honours & Awards
- Projects
- Publications
- Events
- Recommendations
- Groups
- Interests
- 'Stories'

When people visit your profile, LinkedIn wants them to have a good experience – and presumably you do too, so put in some effort to get it as good as it can be.

Finally, write your profile in the first person. When written in the first person, profiles come over as more personable, honest and approachable. Those written in the third person often appear aloof, detached and lacking in the human touch.

Bonus Tip: On the mobile app version of LinkedIn, there is a tool where you can record your name so that people know how to pronounce it when they first talk to you. You have ten seconds of recording time, so with care and thought you could use this to create a ten second elevator pitch.

3. Keywords

As part of fully completing your profile, write down a list of a dozen keywords that sum up your area of expertise.

A 'keyword' can also be a very short phrase such as 'Financial Planning', 'Tax planning', 'Retirement planning for surgeons' etc.

Then, put your list of keywords in order of importance, with the most important keywords at the top of the list.

Then, take the top five keywords on your list and add some or all of them into every section of your LinkedIn profile. Use the remaining keywords in support elsewhere throughout your profile.

Tip: Keep a note of these top five keywords and use them in social media posts across other platforms to maintain consistency of message.

Again, when financial advisers take the time to add their top keywords into carefully thought-through text, they have reported an immediate improvement in their visibility on LinkedIn, with their profile appearing higher in search results, more people viewing their profile and receiving more of the right connection requests.

Pro Tip: Edit/customise your LinkedIn profile URL to include an important keyword. At the very least, edit your

URL to show just your name, rather than the jumble of name and random numbers/letters that LinkedIn gives you.

But consider replacing your name altogether like I have done. Note that I have replaced my name with just keywords:

www.linkedin.com/in/saleskeynotespeaker

By doing this, I am increasing my chances of being found by a conference organiser, meeting planner or training manager who is looking for a sales speaker or trainer.

Note that this is an advanced technique, so think it through carefully before doing something like this with your profile URL.

Bonus Tip: Fully completing your profile also means including your location. People looking for experts on LinkedIn often search by location, so if you do not include it, you may well miss out. So you might include keywords such as:

- Financial planning for surgeons in London
- Mortgage advice for contract workers in Leeds
- Pension planning for CEOs in Manchester

According to LinkedIn, adding your location makes you 23 times more likely to be found in LinkedIn searches…

Also, when you are choosing your keywords, consider adding:

a) Keywords related to the services you offer:

- Financial coaching
- Personal finance podcast
- Retirement planning seminars
- Investment courses
- Cashflow modelling
- Investment advice for high net worth individuals
- Financial life planning
- Mortgage advice
- Etc.

b) Keywords related to your technical skills:

- Tax planning
- Investment planning
- Pension planning
- Employee benefits
- Etc.

c) Keywords related to industries or niches in which you work:

- Healthcare
- Law
- Manufacturing

- Travel
- Food and beverage
- Accounting etc.

d) Keywords related to target Industry buzzwords:

- For example, DB, SIPP, PHI, FCA

Note: Do not include too many buzzwords, because that will put off some people. Focus on the keywords that you know are of interest to your prime target market or ideal client.

e) Keywords related to other business skills that you feel are relevant:

- Leadership
- Teamwork
- Organisation
- Project management
- Strategy
- Customer service
- Presentations
- Etc.

f) You may also want to consider including keywords related to niches or special interests that you have:

- Fishing
- Fine wine
- Fitness
- Art

Finally, when writing your profile **aim it at your perfect, ideal dream client or contact**.

When these people visit your profile, it should:

- Speak directly to them
- Prove that you understand their main problems or issues
- Answer questions that you know are on their mind

When you aim your profile at your perfect client or contact, it will not only appeal to these people, but also to people that are not quite your perfect client/contact, but people who nevertheless you are happy to work with.

4. Your Photo

You MUST have a profile photo. If you don't, you might as well cancel your LinkedIn account.

Really, leave now if you have no intention of having a photo, because countless studies have shown that people just are not interested if you don't have one.

Make sure that your photo is friendly, professional and makes you look trustworthy.

Avoid anything too 'corporate', but equally do not have a photo of you looking too casual – like in your swimming costume on the beach…

And do not use a picture of Batman or James Bond or your dog. Yes, I have seen multiple financial advisers doing this.

Similarly, do not upload your logo instead of a photo. Many people do that, but it dramatically reduces the number of people who will connect with you because the perception is that it is spammy.

Remember, people buy people – not logos.

Also, make sure that your photo is high resolution with a file size up to 8MB. People visiting profiles often click on the photo, so make sure they get to see a great photo of you that is not grainy.

5. Your Cover Photo

Regardless of whether you have standard or premium membership of LinkedIn, you should upload a cover photo. That is the big image at the top of your profile.

Where possible, use an image that reflects something related to your expertise, skills, target market or other activities. For example, if you look at my cover photo, you can see an image of me speaking on a large stage or promoting a book.

www.linkedin.com/in/saleskeynotespeaker

Some people have a different cover image each month – perhaps to reflect the time of year, recent industry awards received or special initiatives. For example, during the early stages of the Coronavirus pandemic, I saw one financial adviser customising her cover image at the top of her profile to highlight that she offered remote/virtual financial advice via Zoom and Skype.

If you use an image editing software tool like Canva, you can also easily overlay some text to add emphasis to what you want to say.

6. Add Photos and Media Throughout Your Profile

This is the sixth tip, and the third to mention photos.

What does that tell you?

Add photos, videos, presentations, PDFs, infographics throughout the about/summary and experience sections. Not everyone wants to read the carefully crafted text on your profile, and some would rather look at pictures. LinkedIn allows a lot of images now, so make the most of this feature. There is even a Featured Image where you can highlight particularly important images.

There is also evidence to suggest that when you add media to your profile, it can help with your visibility on the site and thus increase profile views. I certainly saw a BIG jump in views after I added media to my own profile.

7. Remember Mobile Visitors

One of your best friends when completing your LinkedIn profile is the 'return' key.

Use it to keep sentences on your profile short and also use bullet points to aid clarity. If there is one profession that needs to come across with extreme clarity, it is the financial planning and advice profession.

Not only does this make your profile generally easier to read, but it is particularly helpful to the growing number of people who view LinkedIn on a mobile device.

After initial criticism of LinkedIn's mobile app, they have since put in a lot of work upgrading it – and whilst it is not perfect, its use is growing rapidly amongst LinkedIn's membership. In fact, there are some LinkedIn features which can currently only be accessed through the mobile app.

8. 'Experience' Is not Necessarily Your Previous Job

Most LinkedIn members assume that the Experience section is where you list previous jobs and roles that you have held.

It is, but you can list *anything* in this section.

So perhaps as part of your role or business, you are hosting a webinar. You can list this in your Experience section as a current *activity*. This section is not just for your current job.

Equally, if you ran a series of pensions seminars in your region last summer, you could also add this to your experience section. Whilst they may not have been your actual job, they were an activity as *part* of your job, so can be listed in this section.

For example, on my own profile, my current job is listed as Professional Speaker. But I can also add additional entries listing individual speaking engagements.

How does this help?

It shows that you are active and busy, have value to share – and it helps you to appear in search results when you include some of your keywords.

9. List Your Skills

Don't be shy, use the Skills and Endorsements section to highlight and show off all the areas where you have skills. Visitors to your profile can give you a one-click endorsement.

My personal view is that this feature is a bit clunky, but it is there and you should use it. Also, LinkedIn's algorithm picks up words used in your Skills section when determining search results positioning, so make sure that you include some of your top keywords as skills that you list.

LinkedIn organises your skills as follows:

- Top skills
- Industry knowledge
- Tools & Technologies
- Interpersonal
- Other

'Other' does not have to be work related skills, so show another side of you by including skills like playing the guitar, advanced driving or perhaps watercolour painting etc.

Pro Tip: Technical skills are not everything - when listing your skills, remember to include your SOFT skills too. Hiring managers report that they often find it hard to find people who are 'collaborative', 'adaptable', 'empathetic' etc. simply because LinkedIn members do not include these on their profile.

Periodically, LinkedIn releases a list of the most over-used buzzwords on LinkedIn profiles. Here is the latest list:

- Creative
- Organisational
- Effective
- Extensive experience
- Track record
- Strategic
- Proven sales professional
- Leadership
- Dynamic
- Motivated

- Innovative
- Passionate
- Problem solving
- Expert
- Exceptional communication skills

What do you notice about this list?

That's right, they look like words you would find on a CV.

The problem is, a huge proportion of the LinkedIn membership use words like this in the body of their profile and within the skills section, and as a result find it difficult to stand out from the crowd.

This is another reason to think very carefully about the words and phrases you use on your profile, so that they speak clearly and directly to either your dream connection/client or to your target market.

10. Join Groups

For many people, Groups are the best thing about LinkedIn, because it is here where you can meet, interact and engage with people who have similar interests to you.

These can be work related interests or personal interests that you have. So, for example, if you are into (say) cycling, you will find over 670 groups on LinkedIn that are related to cycling.

These vary from general cycling enthusiasts through to cycling science, cycling jobs, local cycling groups, cycling press, folding bikes enthusiasts and so on.

If you work in the world of cycling, these groups create amazing opportunities to network with others in that field, build relationships, highlight relevant expertise and even grow your list.

Avoid trying to sell within these groups because nobody welcomes it. You might even get kicked out. Simply use the group to draw attention to yourself and your profile through your 'likes', comments and the value you add.

Equally if you cycle for fun and fitness, again you will pick up a wealth of information and tips in these groups.

Having something in common with others is key in business and makes it far easier to build relationships that could lead to doing business together. So financial advisers with a clear client niche, or who are looking to develop a niche can use LinkedIn groups to find and engage with people of interest.

Jared Reynolds - partner in Wilkerson & Reynolds, an advisory firm in Columbia who specialises in working with Bass fishermen is a great example.

Jared has grown his financial planning business by forming a niche working with Bass fishermen, where he arranges fishing and hunting trips, and so gets to spend hours or even days at a time in close proximity with small business owners to form relationships.

(For any financial adviser, it is well worth listening to Michael Kitces' interview with Jared as it gives fantastic insights into the value of working in a niche and how it can be expanded. Check out the Financial Advisor Success podcast interview at www.kitces.com/blog/jared-reynolds-wilkerson-bass-fisherman-niche-passion-prospecting)

If *you* happen to be a financial adviser with an interest in fishing, you can use LinkedIn groups to find other people with a love for the sport.

For example, a search on LinkedIn for 'Fishing' reveals no fewer than 771 groups relating to the topic, giving you more than enough opportunity to start raising your profile in those communities.

Remember, do not sell – engage.

11. Start Your Own Group

Starting your own group on LinkedIn is a big step, but one that can reap many rewards for you over time.

They are another way to build your list – and even if that does not involve acquiring an actual email address, it does mean that you have a group of people who will give you their undivided attention.

The more niche your group is, and the more value that you can add, the better.

To use an aquatic analogy again, treat your group a bit like a fish tank, where the members are the fish. Of course, your fish need feeding every day, so make sure that you add valuable tips, ideas, resources and links (ideally) on a daily basis.

The more great content you post, the more people will want to join and the more engagement there will be. And in turn, the more people will be intrigued by who you are and will want to connect with you.

Although you do not have email addresses for the members of your group*, you can send members an occasional message by highlighting a post of interest. So, you could write a short newsletter as a post in your group and then click a button that will highlight it to members.

Members of your group can also get regular summaries of content in your group, and again LinkedIn will deliver this on your behalf - so make sure that you have added enough content to 'feed' everyone.

Once your group is properly established (and only you will know when that is), you can also OCCASIONALLY make members of your group a direct offer on one of your products and services.

I say 'occasionally' because, however good the content is in your group, you will annoy members if you are constantly promoting and selling stuff.

The idea is to, over time build a reputation for being someone who gives free value – and lots of it. Once that is established, only then should you consider including promotional messages.

It is a difficult balance to get right, but when you do, you will find your conversion rates are extremely high when you do promote an offer. Webinars (free and chargeable) are a great way to take members of your group further up your value ladder.

Groups also have an 'About This Group' tab, so again you can use this any way you wish, though I recommend that you use it to include keywords that are relevant to the group's content, so that it appears in search results.

Finally, a well-run group with great content is a fantastic and proven way to build community around your brand. I have also found that once you have a thriving group, it will inevitably send traffic to your own website when you get the message right.

*There are of course several ways that you can get email addresses for members of your group and drive traffic to your website, and I cover this in my one-to-one Skype/Zoom coaching sessions for financial advisers.

12. Post Status Updates

At the top of the LinkedIn home page, you will see a box that currently says, 'Start a post'. That is the status update box.

What most people do is to post veiled sales pitches or slightly bland content that one way or another links back to their website or company page on LinkedIn. Or they will re-post something similar that someone else has posted.

The worst type of status update says something like:

Check out our latest blog on our website. Click here...
[LINK]

So, it is no surprise that these posts receive very little engagement and are unlikely to result in someone being inspired to look closely at your profile page.

Whilst I am not advocating that you post cat videos on LinkedIn as if it were Facebook, it is important to get people's attention in their news feed.

The secret to great status update posts on LinkedIn which get high views and engagement, is to tell short observational stories about something that that has recently happened in your life or work that either you or others could benefit or learn from.

It could be about someone you met on a train and the conversation you had, or perhaps something strange that happened in a meeting – but ideally it needs to have a human – and thus emotional element.

Avoid including a link to somewhere else in your post, and also avoid including too many images.

That's right, do the opposite of what you would do on Facebook – do not include images. There is a reasonable amount of evidence to suggest that the LinkedIn algorithm is more favourable towards posts that do not include images – unless they are highly emotive and create high initial engagement. That said, the algorithm also seems to favour status updates that include images when the post has been made through the LinkedIn app on a mobile device.

The reason you should not include links, is because the LinkedIn algorithm does not like posts that encourage people to leave LinkedIn, and so your post is shown to far fewer people on the site.

If you must include a link, add your post to LinkedIn *without* the link, and then immediately go back to it, hit 'Edit' and then add in the link. This 'tricks' the LinkedIn algorithm and your post is shown to more people.

You can also add your link to the first comment, and that seems to be OK with the algorithm.

When your post includes human and emotional content, you will inevitably attract Likes and comments, so LinkedIn then shows your post to even more people. The more people who see your post, the greater the likelihood of people visiting your profile page.

Also, aim to post a status update three times a week minimum. Ideally daily. Play around with posting at various times of day to see what gets the best response. You can also try adding the same post at different times of the day to see if that increases traction. In short, split test your posting times.

At first you might find posting so regularly quite challenging and struggle to think of things to post. But after a short while, you start to notice things that would be suitable as you go about your day. You might be crossing the street and suddenly notice something, so keep a note of anything that happens or that you spot which could be used in a post.

The job of your status update is to get people's attention and to stop them scrolling down their news feed. In fact, the longer you can stop someone from scrolling, the more favourable the algorithm will be to your post. LinkedIn calls this Dwell Time and the algorithm rewards posts that:

- Stop people scrolling, even if they don't click on your post
- Stop people scrolling and then click on the post
- Stop people scrolling, click on the post and then Like, Share or Comment on the post

The algorithm increases the reward (greater visibility) the more people engage with your post, so stopping, clicking, liking, sharing and engaging gets the highest reward.

What will stop people from scrolling?

As mentioned before, posts with a highly compelling first sentence and with human, story-based content that ideally includes emotion.

With that in mind, you can now see why posts that just say *'Check out our latest blog on our website. Click here... [LINK]'* are unlikely to be particularly beneficial to you or your business.

13. Post Articles

When the article feature was first introduced on LinkedIn, users found that their content reached thousands of people. I know several people who have attracted speaking, consulting and coaching business straight off the back of an article they posted on LinkedIn.

One person I know in Financial Services posted an article at 08.30 am one morning, and by 11 am had five booked speaking engagements in their inbox.

However, things have changed.

Today, unless you are an 'influencer', your post will generally only reach thousands of people if it has highly emotional content and a killer title. Occasionally LinkedIn's editors will spot an interesting-looking article and give it a boost.

In short, most people who post an article on LinkedIn today will get limited engagement with it.

So why post articles on LinkedIn today?

Firstly, the articles you post will be visible on your LinkedIn profile, so this content adds to how people perceive you. You also get some stats, so you can see what type of content you are posting is getting the best response.

If one article gets a lot more engagement than others, take some time to look closely at it, and figure out how it was different. Then post more like that one.

But more importantly, when you post an article on LinkedIn, you have an option to copy a link to that article to groups that you either run or are a member of, thus extending its reach and potential visibility.

For example, when I post content aimed at financial planners and advisers on LinkedIn, I will post an article on the site and then copy and post the link to it in all the groups where financial advisers hang out. This always results in people visiting my profile.

However, there is another way to use articles on LinkedIn which will not only enhance the perception of your expertise and credibility as a financial professional, but which will also get good volumes of views of your profile.

Firstly, essentially these are the places where you can post content on LinkedIn:

- Status updates
- Articles
- Company pages
- Showcase pages
- Comments on other people's posts
- Groups
- SlideShare
- Advertising
- Events

Status updates are intended for short content and clearly articles are for longer material. However, many people post shorter, lower quality content within articles, so LinkedIn has changed things to encourage high quality submissions within the latter.

For articles to do well, they need to be:

- Long form
- Detailed
- High quality
- In depth

- Analytical
- Research based
- Include unique insights

In addition:

- Write about news in your industry
- Write about timely topics
- Bring your unique expertise to the post that others cannot
- Don't repeat what others are saying
- Give an opinion and provide precise arguments
- Support arguments with industry case studies conducted by credible persons

So, you can see from this that the article section is not for lighter weight content that would be more suitable as status updates.

Articles that go for quality will be favoured by the algorithm, but again human editors at LinkedIn can also give your content a boost. One little-known way to get their attention is to tweet to @LinkedInEditors and invite them to look over your content.

This does not always work, but if your article is of the highest quality, they may well take notice.

In short, posting articles on LinkedIn can be well worth it, as long as you are prepared to put in the effort.

14. Use Hashtags

LinkedIn has reintroduced hashtags, and this can help people to find you when they are using the LinkedIn search tool.

When you post a status update or an article, always include a few relevant hashtags – particularly if those hashtags are also amongst your top keywords.

You can also search for specific hashtags, which will bring up all content that includes that hashtag. So, using the cycling example from earlier, I can search for #cycling and then engage with all relevant content where I can add something of value/interest.

This again draws attention to yourself without selling and sends people to your profile page.

LinkedIn is now rewarding members for engaging with content that includes hashtags, particularly topics where you share an interest with someone else.

Here is what you need to do:

- Search for a hashtag e.g. #Golf

- Save/follow the hashtag #Golf when the search results appear. When you do this, you are signalling to LinkedIn that Golf is a topic of interest to you.

- Scroll down the feed which now only shows content related to Golf.

- Occasionally like and comment on other people's Golf related posts – saying something like *"Great post John, thanks for sharing. #Golf"* or *"Useful post Sue – I'll try that technique next time I'm playing #Golf"*

- When you comment in this way, make sure that your post has at least five words – plus your hashtag

Clearly #Golf is just one example, but you can (and should) also search, follow and engage with other people's content which uses tags of relevance to you, for example #Mortgages, #Pensions, #Investments etc.

What is important to know, is that LinkedIn is now recognising that a huge amount of the content on its platform is made up of people simply broadcasting content and not engaging with one another.

So, they are trying to encourage users to engage with content and other people where they have mutual interests – in this case Golf. And when you do that, LinkedIn will reward you by making you and your content more visible.

15. Know Your Numbers

An important thing about LinkedIn, is to get into a routine with it.

And something you need to do on Mondays is to go to your Notifications stream and look for the message from

LinkedIn that says how many searches you appeared in this week.

Then click on the 'See all searches' button and look at your data. Firstly, if you are not appearing in many searches over the week, it means that you have not completed your profile in as much detail as you should, and that very likely you have not completed the keyword exercise.

Assuming you *are* appearing in search results, with up to and beyond a thousand searches during the week, look at the data and ask yourself if your target market is appearing, along with the keywords they searched. LinkedIn gives you all this data.

After you have done this for a few weeks, you will get a sense for whether or not your profile is appearing in search results for your target market.

If not, tweak your profile, rewrite and keep testing until you are appearing in search results for your exact target audience. Use words and jargon in your profile that your target market uses.

So, for example, if your target market is (say) Accountants, but you are appearing in search results for Graphic Designers, it's likely that your profile needs a rethink.

Hopefully you are beginning to see why your choice of keywords is so important. In many ways, your choice of keywords drives your entire experience of LinkedIn.

16. The Single Most Important Feature on LinkedIn…

Everything we have been talking about so far in this guide has been about behaving in a way on LinkedIn which draws attention to yourself – and specifically *to encourage visits to your profile*.

Everything you do on LinkedIn should be aimed at putting yourself in the best possible light in groups, posts and comments that will encourage people to want to take a closer look.

It is all about creating curiosity.

And here's the thing… no-one ever looks at your LinkedIn profile by accident. They always do it for a reason and on purpose. And it could be just pure curiosity – but that is the point; what we should try to do in all our actions on LinkedIn is to pique someone's curiosity.

The single most valuable feature on LinkedIn tells you whether or not you are succeeding in this mission…

It is the 'Who's Viewed Your Profile' tool, and you currently access it via your profile page.

Now just imagine that you knew the names and details of everyone who visits your website – would that be useful to you?

Yes, of course it would. And that is the wonderful thing about this tool because it shows you who, off their own back, decided to look at your profile.

This information is of course hugely valuable to you. But it's what you do with it that really matters.

Before that, it's worth pointing out that if you have a Basic (free) account on LinkedIn, you will see the five most recent viewers in the last ninety days. Yes, some of them might be in private mode, but if you look at the list every day, you will be pretty well up to date with everyone who has looked at your profile.

When you have a Premium account, you get to see the details of **everyone** who has viewed your profile over the last ninety days (except those in private mode).

Again – know your numbers.

What is this information telling you?

Are the right people looking at your profile?

If not, keep tweaking your profile and your activity on the site until your target audience starts showing up.

Many people ask me if Premium membership is worth having, often arguing that it is expensive for a lot of small business owners.

Clearly if you are an HR Director or have a similar 'big' role in an organisation, then Premium and 'Sales Navigator' have their benefits. But for small business owners and most financial advisers, having this one feature of being able to see the full list of your profile viewers makes Premium worth having.

That said, even knowing just the last five people who looked at your profile could be the difference between getting a job or not, making a valuable new connection or winning/losing a great new client.

17. Say Hello…!

So, people are visiting your profile page. That's great news! We're making progress…

And hopefully we are constantly tweaking our profile to make it as relevant as possible to our target audience. Any of the following could result in someone visiting your profile:

- Search result
- Status update seen
- Article seen
- Profile update
- Activity in a group seen
- Like, share or comment seen
- You looked at someone's profile
- You followed someone
- You mentioned or tagged someone in a post
- Comment on a company page
- Comment on a showcase page
- Promotion outside LinkedIn
- Google search result
- It's your birthday
- Job anniversary
- New job/role
- Promotion
- They follow a hashtag you used

Now what?

Someone once told me that 99% of LinkedIn users never bother to say 'hello' or 'thank you' to people who visit their profile. I don't know if that figure is correct, but in my own experience it is bang on.

Why is this important?

If people took the trouble to look at your profile, they did it for a reason, so let's try to find out and see where it leads us...

18. Thank People Who Have Looked at Your Profile

We're going to look at scripts in more detail at the end of this guide, but in the meantime, here's the exact script that I use when following up after someone has looked at my profile; and I send it as a connection request if they are not already in my LinkedIn network:

"Hi [Name]...

Thanks for taking a look at my profile today – I hope you found something of interest...

Optional but recommended extra to build rapport >> *[I noticed that we're both in the XYZ Cycling group!]* or *[I see that we have mutual connections in Sue Smith and John Jones]*

Please do let me know if I can introduce you to anyone in my network – in the meantime it would be great to connect please.

Thanks in advance [Name]...

Phil"

A few things to note:

My success rate at connecting with people using that script is well in excess of 90%. Sometimes it is nearer 100%

I have financial adviser clients who told me that they got amazing new pension and investment enquiries *the very first time* they used this technique.

I do not follow up *everyone* who visits my profile – you should look through the list of your viewers and use common sense as to who might be worth following up.

For example, I'm a professional speaker, and if a meeting planner or conference organiser looks at my profile, I will definitely follow them up.

Now this is important...

Do NOT go into sales mode if your perfect/dream customer shows up. Remember, all they did was look at your profile, so what we are trying to do now is start a conversation; nothing else. Hopefully that conversation will lead to a coffee.

Note in my message that I offered to help to broaden their network by connecting them to someone in my own network. This is a GIVING activity and people welcome it even if they don't take up the offer.

Our message/communication must seek to GIVE, not TAKE or sell. You will notice that there isn't the slightest hint of a sales message in my contact request.

Use the words *"Thanks in advance..."*. I have seen research that suggests these words (complete with the ellipses/three dots), increases the likelihood of a favourable response.

Most important of all, ALWAYS customise the message with their name – ideally at the start and the end of the message.

When using their name at the start of the message, include the ellipses "..." after their name. This encourages people to keep reading. Out of the corner of their eye, they will also see their name further down the message – again this will encourage people to keep reading.

19. Connect with People You Have Found Through Search

Here is the script that I use when I want to connect with people that I have found on LinkedIn – perhaps through search, in a group or elsewhere:

"Hi [Name]...

I was excited to find your profile on LinkedIn today. I see that we have mutual connections in John Jones and Sue Smith, and it would be great to connect please.

Or, instead of having mutual connections:

I noticed that we're both in the XYZ Cycling group on LinkedIn! or *I see that we [have something else in common] and it would be great to connect please.*

Thanks in advance [Name]...

Phil"

Points to note:

Never connect with people through the Connect button in the 'People You May Know' section.

Yes, connect with them by all means, but only do it via the Connect button on their profile page, otherwise you will not be able to customise the message.

And again, you need to look at their profile first so that you can find something of interest that you have in common.

The secret with connecting is finding something that you have in common – however small.

My Dad told me that 'people buy people' and that's as true online as it is face to face, so always look for the human-interest connection – be it cycling (or whatever), mutual connections, location, group membership or something else. You can usually find something.

I once got a big speaking engagement simply because I had a mutual interest in kickboxing with someone I found on LinkedIn.

Yes, it works…

20. Get Even More Profile Views – Pro Tip

It is a simple fact that the more people's profiles you look at, the more will look at yours. And that's good news, right?!

Yes, human nature has a part to play.

You can leverage this by either spending time searching for ideal customers and visiting their profiles - or as some people suggest automating it.

There are several tools available that will automate visits to profiles several hundred at a time, and even send connection requests.

This has advantages and some (big) disadvantages. The advantages are obvious, but the disadvantages can be as bad as getting kicked off LinkedIn or sin-binned for a period.

These automation tools can be extremely useful but must be used with a great deal of care. For starters, if you are on the free version of LinkedIn, there is a 'commercial use' limit which is designed to stop spammers, but also to encourage bone fide heavy users to pay. E.g. recruiters etc.

LinkedIn will not tell you what your commercial use limit is, so it is best to use such tools **very sparingly**. If you suddenly go from doing very few searches a week to several hundred a day, the LinkedIn system will pick you up, so if you do use this approach, build it up very gradually over several weeks.

Many LinkedIn heavy users like me, find occasional automation incredibly valuable – but don't tell me you have not been warned…!

I tend to use an automation tool about once a month if that – perhaps when I'm searching for a very specific type of person. The tool I use will visit the profiles for me and then I go into manual mode when people start looking at my profile.

I would advise against using automation tools to send connection requests (even personalised with names) because you run the risk of too many not accepting your request, which again could lead to LinkedIn blocking your account for a while. In short, always do connection messages manually as described in #18 and #19 above.

To summarise, automation tools occasionally have their place, but LinkedIn frowns upon it and will block your account or similar if you abuse the system – and there is evidence to suggest that they are getting much tougher.

I include this tip, because there are many people suggesting that you use automation tools – or offer to do it for you. In short, I am hearing more and more that this is not a good idea, so if you must use automation, do so with extreme care.

Bonus tip on automation:

However, whilst not strictly an automation tool, there is a *fantastic* service that I use called VERY FAST.

Rather than automate the sending of messages, VERY FAST significantly speeds up the time it takes to send *personalised* messages that you were going to send anyway.

Simply what it does, is to allow you to create a series of template messages that you might want to send to people. The tool also personalises the messages with their name.

So for example, you could create template messages for:

- Replying to people who want to connect with you
- Sending connection request messages to other people
- Sending messages to unconnected people who have looked at your profile
- Sending messages to people who you are already connected with who have looked at your profile

- Sending messages to people who have wished you Happy Birthday
- Sending messages to people who have congratulated you on a new job or role
- Sending your own messages of congratulations to other people
- Sending messages of thanks to people who have endorsed you for one of your listed skills
- Welcoming people who want to join your LinkedIn group
- Sending messages to someone you might want to interview or recruit
- Sending follow up messages to prospects
- Sending messages to direct people to your website, funnel, special offer or free download
- Etc.

You can also send template messages to specific types of people who have done any of the above. So for example, you could send different messages depending on certain niches in which you operate or target.

Perhaps you target (say) Accountants or Surgeons with your products or services, so you can create a personalised template, each with a slightly different message depending on their industry.

As at the time of writing, the service is still in Beta, but to date it has saved me many hours of time.

Prior to using it, I would create template messages on a Word document or similar, and then copy and paste a message into LinkedIn, remembering of course to personalise it.

With VERY FAST, the whole thing is done in the blink of an eye.

The site is to be found at https://getveryfast.com

Oh, and it is (currently) free...

21. Remove Distractions (Such as Your Competitors) From Your Profile Page...

One of the problems with LinkedIn, is that they proactively encourage you to connect with people. That's not a problem in itself - it is just that one of the places where they do that is on your profile page!

Have you noticed that when you visit someone's profile page on LinkedIn, usually on the right side it says, 'People Also Viewed'. Now if you work for a larger company, the people in that list are more than likely to be your colleagues or people in other companies in similar roles to you - or with similar skills and experience.

This can cause you problems if you are a) hoping that a recruiter will contact you about possible job opportunities, and b) if you are self-employed or have your own business.

If you are looking for a job and have flagged that up on LinkedIn (there's a tool where you can alert recruiters to your availability), when recruiters or potential employers visit your profile, if they see a list on the right side that says 'People Also Viewed', they know that these are people who have similar skills to you - and they may well include them in their search. The list might even distract them altogether from your profile!

Equally, if you are a financial adviser, when someone visits your profile to check you out - the last thing you want them to see on your profile, is a list of other financial advisers. In short, the people in the list on the right are more than likely to be your competitors!

The good news is that within your LinkedIn privacy settings, you can turn off this feature. And I strongly suggest that you do that!

Yes, your profile is all about YOU. Do not let people visiting your profile get distracted by others who they might be tempted to talk to first...

LinkedIn Connection Scripts

When using LinkedIn, it's important to remember that we are not looking to do business with someone straight off your LinkedIn profile. It does occasionally happen, but it is extremely unlikely that someone will find our profile and make an immediate request to purchase our products or services.

What we are aiming to do through LinkedIn messages, is little more than to **start a conversation**.

These scripts include proven copywriting techniques, so try to avoid altering them too much - but feel free to model and customise them to your proposed connection's interests.

When the conversation is going in the right direction, look to build the relationship off LinkedIn in the traditional way. I.e. on the phone, on Zoom, over coffee etc.

How to thank people who are not connections and who have looked at your profile

Hi John…

Thanks for taking a look at my profile page – I hope you found something of interest [?]

I noticed that we have some mutual connections, and it would be great to connect please.

Thanks in advance…

Philip

On the surface this looks like a remarkably simple script, but there is more to it than meets the eye.

- Send this message as a connection request.

- Always use their name as it shows you are potentially not a spammer. What is more it is polite and will help with trust etc.

- Add "…" after their name because this hints to them that there is more to follow.

- Say *"thank you"* because it is polite and everyone likes to be thanked. If you have a real-life store, it's always good to say thank you to people for stopping by.

- The "?" is optional.

- Always try to say something that shows/proves that you have something in common. This is immediately appealing to most people. Just having mutual connections will normally be sufficient, but if it is clear from their profile that they and you both play golf, then refer to that.

    If you have mutual connections within a specific industry, refer to that. E.g. *"I see that we have mutual connections in the Accountancy world"*

- Finish with *"Thanks in advance…"*. I have found by split testing over time, that this phrase dramatically increases the likelihood that they will reply (or accept your request).

Someone asked to connect with you: V1

Assuming that you want to accept their request:

Hi Sue…

Yes! I'm very happy to connect – thank you and I appreciate your interest. [Optional: Welcome to my network!]

Please let me know if I can connect you to anyone in my network.

Can I ask what prompted you to say hello?

Thanks in advance…

Philip

- 99% of these requests will not have been personalised but reply as if they had been.

- One of the most important parts of this is the statement *"Please let me know if I can connect you to anyone in my network"* because huge numbers of people go straight into sales mode at this point. So, what you should do is the exact opposite. You do this by offering to give them something of potentially very high value. i.e. a useful connection.

In reality, hardly anyone takes you up on this, but you are using the law of reciprocity to make it much more likely that they will give you something back – even if it is an exchange of messages – which is exactly what we want.

- Very often they will reply to the question *"Can I ask what prompted you to say hello?"* and I have attracted business on many occasions by asking it in this message.

Someone asked to connect with you: V2

This is what I send to financial advisers who ask to connect with me:

Hi Michael...

Yes! I'm very happy to connect – thank you. I see that you are a [Financial Planner]?

The majority of my [financial services] connections have joined my private forum. Almost 2,000 of them use it to share useful resources and to make valuable connections – you should join us...

Financial Planners are joining here [www.facebook.com/groups/AdviserLifeTalk]. And it's free!

Thanks in advance...

Philip

This is a bit more advanced because we are using LinkedIn and your message as the top of your funnel – driving them to some value that is highly relevant to them.

This pre-supposes that your LinkedIn plan is deliberately set up to attract specific types of people you want to work with – in this case financial advisers.

You will also note that the message includes social proof *"Financial Planners are joining here"*, and this serves to make the offer even more attractive.

When financial advisers ask to connect with me on LinkedIn, almost 100% of them go on to join my group.

Also note the words *"It's free"*, which just make it a no-brainer for them to join.

Someone followed you (instead of connecting with you)

Hi Jim...

Thank you! I appreciate you following my profile – I hope you'll find something of interest. [Optional: I see that we both are connected to John etc]

Please let me know if I can introduce you to anyone in my network. Can I ask what prompted you to follow my posts?

Thanks in advance...

Philip

You want to connect with someone

Hi Peter…

I spotted you on LinkedIn today and noticed that we have mutual connections in the [Accountancy] world.

It would be great to connect please.

Thanks in advance…

Philip

Again, a really simple message using the techniques mentioned earlier.

One of the key parts is the phrase:

"I spotted you on LinkedIn"

…which suggests that you discovered them as a result of something *they did* on the site.

If you are able to personalise the message even further, then all the better.

For example:

Hi Peter…

I spotted you on LinkedIn today and noticed that we have a mutual interest in [Yoga]! How often do you practice?

It would be great to connect please.

Thanks in advance…

Philip

Or:

Hi Mary…

It was great to meet you at the conference today and I just spotted you on LinkedIn. What did you think of today's event?

It would be great to connect please.

Thanks in advance…

Philip

When they accept your request

Hi again Maria...

Great! Thanks for connecting – I appreciate your interest.

If I can connect you to anyone in my network, please don't hesitate to ask.

- *I noticed your post about [topic] and it caught my attention.*
- *I see that you are also connected to [James Smith]*
- *I see that you are based in [Cambridge]. It must be great working there!*
- *I'm doing a bit of research at the moment for a project - what is the biggest issue that [Financial Planners] are struggling with right now? I'd be keen on your thoughts*

Thanks in advance...

Philip

The bulleted points are suggestions – pick one or write something that will engage with the person concerned.

Key points in LinkedIn connection messages

- Always use their name

- Try to find things that you have in common, and refer to them in your message

- Offer something valuable that they won't be expecting. E.g. an introduction to someone in your network

- Never try to sell anything

- When you do point them to something of yours, it MUST be high value, free and directly relevant to their world. Through social proof, highlight that other people like them have already taken action

- All we are doing is starting a conversation. We are NOT going anywhere near 'sales mode' at this point. Save that for when the time is right and only you will know when that is.

By way of a practical example, financial advisers often tell me that they get a lot of recruiters wanting to connect with them, and whilst most are not interested in connecting with them, some have turned it round to their advantage with this message:

Hi Tim...

Thanks for taking a look at my profile today – I see that you are in Recruitment? Please let me know if there is anyone in my network that I could introduce you to.

In the meantime, recruiters are downloading our guide "Ten Easy Ways for Recruitment Professionals to Increase Their Income in Retirement". It's free!

Recruiters are downloading it at www.mywebsite.com

Thanks in advance...

Mary

So, in this example you can see several of the messaging elements coming together in one communication. Model and adapt it to your own target market. The more niche you can make it, the better.

Networking like a Pro: Networking questions that build relationships online and offline

I hope that you have found this book of interest, but I wanted to finish Part 1 by making a vital point, and that is to stress the fact that LinkedIn is about Social *Networking* and not Social *Media*. It is an important difference.

Yes, on the surface LinkedIn looks like Social Media, and yes, many people use it that way. But if you want success on the site, remember that it is fundamentally a tool to help people to network with each other.

The more that you use it to interact and engage with people in a professional and human way, the more value you and they will get from it.

But many people simply do not know how to network, believing that networking is about meeting people, exchanging business cards and asking for business.

The worst type of networkers are the people who arrive early at a networking event and put a business card on every chair, in the hope that someone will get in touch. This *is not* networking.

The best type of networking is where you go out of your way to help other people through your own network of contacts, and without any expectation of anything in return.

I am going to finish this section with three questions that I use in any networking situations, which have served me well over many years.

Instead of *"What do you do?"* ask *"What is your area of expertise?"*

Then ask, *"What are you working on in your business at the moment that you are really excited about?"*

Or *"What big projects are you working on [in your business] at the moment?"*

And then *"Who could I connect you to who could help you with that?"*

Or

"What additional expertise would be useful to you if I could introduce you to someone who could help [who could bring the project in faster, cheaper etc]?"

As you can see, these questions are all about the other person and not about you. Listen carefully to their answers and get back to them as quickly as possible with a connection from your network.

Even if you do not have someone that you could introduce them to, get back to them anyway and keep the relationship plates spinning for another day. Either way, they will not forget you and one day they may well reciprocate by referring you to someone else.

If you use LinkedIn in much the same way – i.e. to help people by introducing them to people you know, you will find your experience of the site dramatically enhanced.

So far so good...

There is of course more to LinkedIn than we have been able to cover here, but what you have is literally the cheat sheet to getting it right on LinkedIn as a financial adviser – and you can see that almost all of this can be done without paying for Premium.

In Part 2, we are going to put it into action with specific steps that financial advisers should take – including a lead generation planner and activity journal.

PART 2

Your LinkedIn Lead Generation Planner and Journal

Contents

Introduction

Planning

Recommended actions

Getting started – the Five Golden areas of daily activity

Part 1

Part 2

Part 3

Part 4

Part 5

Optional additional activity

Compliance

Daily Planner and Journal

About the Author

Disclaimer and Terms of Use

Introduction to Part Two

This combined book, planner and journal is for any IFA, financial adviser, RIA or wealth manager who hopes and believes that LinkedIn is a potential powerhouse of opportunity for their business.

You are in luck – it is!

At every single workshop I run, or conference speech that I give to financial advisers around the world, I am always asked what the best way is to attract new leads through LinkedIn.

Whilst Facebook continues to be all dominant in the social media space, LinkedIn is receiving significantly increased attention – so much so that business owners and entrepreneurs all round the world are more eager than ever to include it at the heart of their sales and marketing activities.

But very few financial advisers use LinkedIn strategically, so they are missing out on a potential goldmine. This section of the book will help them to get much better focus on the key activities that attract new leads – and without paying for advertising.

And the good news is that I have had financial advisers tell me that they attracted high quality new investment and pensions clients the very first time they used the LinkedIn techniques I teach.

So, thanks for your interest in this LinkedIn Planner and Journal – I hope that you will enjoy completing it and get a lot of value from recording your day to day experience on the site.

The sole purpose of this part of the book is to **help you to attract more of the clients and connections that you really want on LinkedIn.** Nothing more and nothing less.

As LinkedIn nears 700 million members, the site offers a wealth of opportunity for financial advisers, but like any other software that you use in your business, you will only see real benefits when you know how to use it properly and strategically.

I have been on LinkedIn right from the start, and I speak and train on LinkedIn lead generation around the world. This section of the book builds on Part 1 and provides a straightforward, no fluff planner which shares a simple and proven process which works time and time again for me and my clients.

It is part planner and part journal, giving you the opportunity to get focus on *why* you are using LinkedIn, and also to share *what you are doing* and the results you are getting.

The better your planning, the better potential you have for getting the results you want. And the more you document your activity, the more you will see patterns in what you do on LinkedIn and how it relates to the results you are achieving.

You should also join our accompanying group **Marketing for Financial Advisers** where you will discover a wealth of additional LinkedIn tips, tricks and strategies to help you achieve your goals.

Join us at https://www.financialadvice.marketing

Planning

Before going any further, it is really important that you have a clear idea on **why** you are using LinkedIn in the first place.

The vast majority of financial advisers on LinkedIn waste a great deal of time 'floundering' around on the platform without having a clear idea of what they are trying to achieve.

Each time they log in to the site or app, they move around without any clear direction or purpose, so the point of this section is to give you a clear strategy and approach.

For most financial advisers on LinkedIn, whether employed or self-employed, the best outcome will usually result from people visiting your profile.

You therefore need to:

1. Create and position your LinkedIn profile so that it **speaks directly to your ideal client** or connection

2. Draw attention from the LinkedIn algorithm so that **it supports, rewards and promotes you and your expertise**

3. Draw attention from your ideal client or connection **so that they want to visit your profile**

4. Engage with people who visit your profile **in a way that starts conversations**

The tips in this section are designed to help you easily achieve all of the above. But first, let's build on the short exercise we did earlier, and get some clarity on **why** you are on LinkedIn by answering the following questions:

Describe yourself and your financial advice business

_____
_____
_____
_____
_____
_____
_____
_____
_____
_____

Describe your **ideal** client or connection – the ones you **really** want

_____
_____
_____
_____
_____
_____
_____

_____
_____
_____
_____

Why are you targeting these people and what problems do they have that you can solve?

_____
_____
_____
_____
_____
_____
_____
_____
_____
_____

How many of them are on LinkedIn? (Hint: use the search tool)

_____
_____
_____
_____
_____
_____
_____
_____

_____
_____
_____

What do they post status updates about?

_____
_____
_____
_____
_____
_____
_____
_____
_____

What articles do they post on LinkedIn and what themes/topics do they cover?

_____
_____
_____
_____
_____
_____
_____
_____
_____

What hashtags are they using with their posts and comments?

What LinkedIn groups have they joined?

Do they have LinkedIn Company Pages, and if so, what content do they post there?

_____
_____
_____
_____
_____
_____
_____
_____
_____
_____

Do they have a Showcase Page on LinkedIn and if so, what do they post about there?

_____
_____
_____
_____
_____
_____
_____
_____
_____
_____
_____

Are they promoting any events on LinkedIn and if so what type of events are they promoting?

_____
_____
_____
_____
_____
_____
_____
_____
_____
_____
_____
_____

What is your **primary** area of expertise?

_____
_____
_____
_____
_____
_____
_____
_____
_____
_____
_____
_____

What is your ideal result from using LinkedIn and how does that help you to achieve your goals for the year/next five years etc?

_____
_____
_____
_____
_____
_____
_____
_____
_____
_____
_____
_____

What did you notice about these questions?

Yes, they are more about understanding how your target market uses LinkedIn than about yourself.

It goes without saying that not all your ideal clients will be on LinkedIn, but if you target anyone between the age of 25 and 65 who is either employed or self-employed, they are likely to be on the site. Don't forget also that many people stay on LinkedIn for a few years after they have retired, so they may well be there too.

When you really get to know your ideal connections on LinkedIn, you are giving yourself a significantly improved chance of attracting more of the leads and clients that you really want. **It also helps to focus the mind on posting content that is relevant to their needs.**

Answering these questions often forces people to think much more clearly about how they use LinkedIn to attract their ideal connections, and you will find that almost straight away you will have more focus in your use of the site.

So far so good...

Recommended actions before starting your LinkedIn Daily Planner

Next, there are certain hygiene factors that we need to put in place – not least of which is that your personal LinkedIn profile needs to be fit for purpose.

Just like when building a house, you need to start with the foundations.

1. Financial Advisers should have a **fully completed personal profile** that is keyword optimised throughout and it should have been written to address the primary problems, needs or characteristics of your main target market.

2. You should also have searched for and followed up to ten hashtags that are used by or are highly relevant to your target market. Go to LinkedIn home and search (for example) #Retirement and then click the Follow button. Follow other hashtags that you know are of interest to your target market. E.g. #Golf.

3. You should also have joined any special interest groups on LinkedIn where your target market hangs out. Don't forget that these will also include groups related to their work, business or personal interests – not necessarily personal finance related.

For example, there are over 3,000 groups on LinkedIn for people interested in golf; almost 3,000 related to football and around 80 related to fishing. There are over 28,000 groups related to leadership and most of these groups have memberships in the thousands.

4. You should also have created and optimised your Company Page on LinkedIn.

Useful but not essential:

1. Signed up for Premium membership
2. Created a Showcase page on LinkedIn

Note: Nothing I am about to describe requires the use of LinkedIn Premium membership.

As mentioned in Part 1, Premium membership's key benefit in the context of lead generation is that with the free version you are able to see the last five people who looked at your profile, and with Premium, you can see everyone who has looked at you over the last ninety days.

So if you log in every day, you will over time be fully up to speed on who is looking at your profile. Keep reading to understand why this is so important.

Getting Started

The Golden Five areas of activity each day

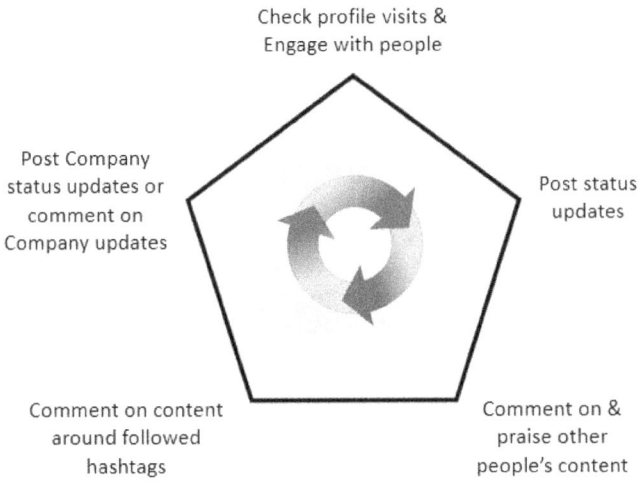

Your ideal daily LinkedIn activity is divided into five parts:

1. Check profile visits and engage with people – send and reply to messages – make and accept connection requests

2. Post status updates

3. Comment on other people's content

4. Comment on content around followed hashtags

5. Post Company status updates or comment on Company updates

Let's look at each in turn.

GOLDEN FIVE ACTIVITY 1

Profile Visits and Engaging with People

People who visit your profile have done so deliberately. (Note: It is possible that it will have been an automated visit using external software tools, but the vast majority of visits to your profile will have been done manually by the person themselves as a result of finding you on LinkedIn.)

These visits to your profile represent a valuable opportunity to **start conversations** that begin through the LinkedIn messaging system, but which progress to email, telephone, Skype/Zoom or a meeting in a coffee shop.

In my view, the feature which shows who has visited your profile is one of, if not *the* most powerful tool on LinkedIn to start the process of generating new leads and enquiries.

To maximise the likelihood of conversations taking place, you should follow this approach:

First, check who viewed your LinkedIn profile and then look at their profile.

As you look at their profile consider:

- What do you both have in common?
- Why do you think they looked at you?
- Say 'thank you' to them by sending a personalised connection request if not already connected*

- Say 'thank you' to them if you are already connected: "*What prompted you to stop by?*"

*I have had financial advisers tell me that they attracted high value new investment and pension clients the **very first time** they said 'thank you' to strangers who visited their profile.

Consider using scripts – here is a reminder of the two main ones from Part 1:

Script 1

Hi Sue…

Many thanks for taking a look at my profile – I see that we have some mutual connections. Please let me know if I can introduce you to anyone else in my network.

In the meantime, it would be great to connect.

Thanks in advance…

Regards

Phil

Script 2

Hi Sue…

Many thanks for taking a look at my profile again – I hope you found something of interest and that things are going well for you.

May I ask what prompted you to drop by?

Thanks in advance...

Regards

Phil

In many cases, people will actually reply to you, so you should then take the opportunity to engage with them in conversation – building on any areas of common interest.

If they accept your connection request but do not reply, send another message thanking them for connecting, and politely asking what prompted them to connect.

Want to stand out from the crowd?

Once you are connected to someone, if enabled on your LinkedIn app, you will be able to not only send written messages, but also audio and video messages to people.

This is a powerful and proven way for financial advisers to differentiate themselves, because very few people use these messaging features on LinkedIn.

Again, avoid being self-promotional in these messages. Your aim is to **engage with people with a view to starting a conversation.** Leave the salesy stuff to further down the line when the relationship is maturing.

GOLDEN FIVE ACTIVITY 2

Status Updates

Each day, post a short observational or story-based status update around something you did, noticed, thought about, watched, heard etc. over the last twenty-four hours. Try to avoid including a hyperlink to somewhere that is off LinkedIn e.g. your blog or website.

Status Updates are designed to draw people's attention to you so that they go on to look at your profile.

Follow these tips to maximise potential from the LinkedIn algorithm:

- Avoid making your post promotional

- Try to write your content so that it encourages interaction and conversations between readers, so occasionally ask a question at the end of your post. 'Engagement probability' is an important driver of the LinkedIn algorithm

- Occasionally post about news within the financial planning industry – or news within your target market's industry

- Occasionally use infographics to highlight points you are making

- Occasionally go deep and niche on topics in your posts

- Remember that 'people buy people', so aim for human content occasionally – include emotion, humour, nostalgia etc.

- Highlight your expertise without selling – include short tips, inside information and case studies. Educational content is great too.

- Post content that you know your target audience cares about. How relevant your content is to them is a key driver of the LinkedIn algorithm.

- Occasionally tag companies and individuals in your posts – more as a way to highlight their skills, expertise and services rather than to get their attention.

  As a financial adviser, occasionally you might want to mention or tag local professional connections

- Publicly thank people for their help – use the LinkedIn Kudos tool. There is also the ability through a dedicated button in the status update space to share and highlight an individual's profile.

- Use native and live video as posts

- Post about events that you have attended or that you are at right now

- Include three relevant hashtags on your post

- Monitor which times of day get the most engagement on your posts

Here's an example of a story-based status update of my own that I posted on LinkedIn a little while ago:

"An hour ago I checked the price of parking at Gatwick airport as I'm speaking in Bulgaria next week and unfortunately I've left it a bit late in the day to book my car in. Their site quoted me £27.50 for two days parking.

Before booking it, I needed to go to the post office and then get a haircut.

I've just got back in after running my errands, sat down to book the parking and I'm now being quoted £52!

D'oh!

#shouldhavebookeditearlier"

Here's how that seemingly innocuous little post performed:

- 1,230 likes
- 227 comments
- 26% increase in profile views over the week
- 23 direct messages, that resulted in…
- 23 conversations

As you can see, the post didn't promote any products or services, didn't include a link to anything and didn't include any images. It was just a short, simple, observation on a part of daily life that many of us can associate with.

It's also slightly self-deprecating and has a hint of humour. And it took all of thirty seconds to write.

Hopefully, this is a useful example of how easy it is to get profile views which lead to conversations.

How could I have improved engagement even more?

I didn't really have time when I posted it, but If I had thought about it in a little more detail, I could also have tagged Gatwick Airport's Company page on LinkedIn, and that would have attracted some attention from them as well.

Again, in hindsight I should have added "#Bulgaria" as a hashtag in the post and that would have got attention from LinkedIn users in that country. A search on LinkedIn shows that there are over 8,400 Bulgarian companies or business interests on the site.

There are also 700,000 profiles on LinkedIn belonging to people who either work in Bulgaria or who have some connection to the country.

"#Bulgaria" has been used over 27,000 times on LinkedIn and over 2,400 people actually follow that hashtag – so again, with a little more thought I could have got even more engagement on my post.

Thinking about it now, I probably missed out on further speaking and training opportunities simply because I didn't use the #Bulgaria hashtag.

Food for thought, yes?!

Notes:

Aim for a minimum of one status update *every* weekday, but three spread over a day is even better. You can also post the same update more than once a day – make a note of which one gets the most traction.

Consider posting at weekends too, though not essential.

Share your post to Twitter. This can be automated if you have included your Twitter information in your contact details.

Time required per post: one to three minutes – possibly longer if you need to create a fancy infographic.

Plan your posts in advance if you have time.

Take note of what LinkedIn themselves say:

"Genuine conversation around real experiences spark better and deeper conversation. Better conversation, in turn, leads to stronger community and connection."

GOLDEN FIVE ACTIVITY 3

Comment on other people's posts on the main home news feed

By commenting on other people's posts, you are sending a signal to the LinkedIn algorithm that you are a networker and not a broadcaster, and as a result you will be rewarded with greater visibility, and more often than not, more profile visits.

Remember, every time you comment on someone else's posts, you are providing them and their followers and contacts with a direct link to your profile.

Here is what you should do:

- Scroll through your news feed and pick out interesting content from other people – particularly people in your prime target market or their industry/profession

- Avoid salesy comments – keep it simple and post things such as *"Great post Sue – thanks for the heads up"* or *"Thanks for the useful insights John – extremely valuable"*

- Do not post anything self-promotional

- Add up to three relevant hashtags to your comments. So in the example above, your comment might look something like this:

"Thanks for the useful insights John – extremely valuable. #retirement #lifestyle"

- If you really do not have any comments to make, then 'Like' other people's posts – even this will help draw attention to you

Notes:

Add comments to three posts each day. More if you can.

Time required per comment: 30 seconds max.

GOLDEN FIVE ACTIVITY 4

Comment on other people's posts that revolve around a saved/followed hashtag

LinkedIn is conscious that far too many people simply broadcast content on the platform, so the LinkedIn algorithm is now rewarding people who **interact and engage with others around areas of common interest**.

Follow the actions below, and you will send a message to the LinkedIn algorithm that you are a networker and not a broadcaster.

Yes, broadcasting has its place, but if you want more people to visit your profile so that you can start conversations, you should play the LinkedIn game and follow their rules.

When you do, you will be rewarded with greater visibility and more profile visits. Your comments will also be more visible to other people who follow specific hashtags.

Remember again - every time you comment on someone else's posts, you are providing them and their followers and contacts with a direct link to your profile.

Here is what you should do:

- Visit your list of saved/followed hashtags. On mobile, tap on your photo on the home feed; this opens a side bar where you will find your followed hashtags. On desktop, your followed hashtags are on the left side of your home screen (both these may be subject to change by LinkedIn).

- Tap/click on a hashtag used by your target audience.

- Scroll down the news feed for that hashtag and add short comments such as *"Great post Sue – thanks for the heads up"* or *"Thanks for the useful insights John – extremely valuable"*.

- Do not post anything self-promotional in your comments.

- Add up to three relevant hashtags to your comment – ideally one of which is the hashtag that you are currently viewing. So if you are commenting on a post in the feed for (say) #Leadership, you could post something like:

    "Thanks for sharing Susan – you've made some great points there. #Leadership #Management #Change"

- If you really do not have any comments to make, then 'Like' other people's posts – even this will help draw attention to you. But commenting is always the best course of action.

Notes:

Add comments to three posts each day. More if you can.

Time required per comment: 30 seconds max.

GOLDEN FIVE ACTIVITY 5

Company Status Updates

Post a short observational or story-based status update around something you did, noticed, thought about, watched, heard etc. over the last twenty-four hours. Try to avoid including a hyperlink to somewhere that is off LinkedIn e.g. your blog or website.

Tips:

- Try to follow a theme in your posts that is related to your company's expertise – perhaps have a weekly or monthly theme.

- Avoid making your post promotional, though one, maybe two posts per week that are purely promotional is fine.

- Try to write your content so that it encourages interaction and engagement by readers, so occasionally ask a question at the end of your post.

- Occasionally post about news in your industry.

- Occasionally use infographics to highlight points you are making.

- Remember that 'people buy people' (even on Company Pages), so aim for human content occasionally – include emotion, humour, nostalgia etc.

- Show your expertise without selling – include short tips, inside information, educational content and client case studies.

- Occasionally tag companies, individuals, colleagues, suppliers and professional introducers in your posts – more as a way to highlight their skills, expertise and services rather than to get their attention.

- Publicly thank people for their help – perhaps a local professional connection.

- Use native and live streaming video as posts.

- Post about events that you have attended or that you are at right now. Make these a mixture of local events, your own events and financial services industry events (there is no shortage of them!)

- Include three relevant hashtags on your post.

- If you are not the Admin for your own Company page, you should still comment on posts that others have written.

Notes:

Aim for a minimum of one Company Page status update per day, every weekday - but three spread over a day is even better.

Consider posting at weekends too, though not essential.

Time required per post: one to three minutes – possibly longer if you need to create a fancy infographic. Longer if you are streaming a live video.

Live streaming video on Company Pages is highly recommended and can *dramatically* increase views.

Note: You need to apply to be a 'LinkedIn Live Broadcaster' and you can do that here: https://www.linkedin.com/help/linkedin/ask/lv-app

If you have colleagues, make a point of telling them that something has been posted on your Company Page, and encourage them to Like, Comment and Share your posts so that your reach on LinkedIn is significantly extended.

Plan your posts in advance if you have time.

Optional Additional Daily Activity

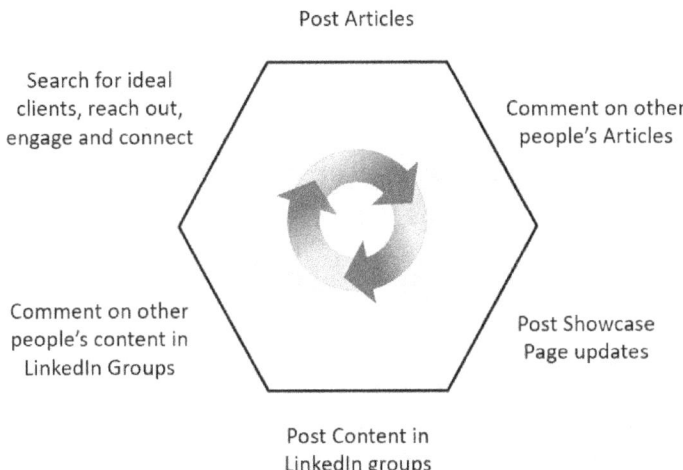

The Golden Five daily activities I have just described are what really matter for financial advisers when trying to attract your ideal clients and connections on LinkedIn, but there is more that you can do to support your core activity if you have time.

Such as:

- Post articles
- Comment on other people's articles
- Post Showcase page updates
- Post content in LinkedIn groups
- Comment on other people's content in LinkedIn Groups

- Search for ideal clients, reach out, engage and connect

Notes:

As mentioned earlier, for maximum traction your own articles need to be long, detailed, deep on expertise, niche, factual and include unique insights. Therefore these are time-consuming but potentially high value.

Showcase Page updates should follow the same approach as Company Page updates.

Avoid self-promotional content in Groups – aim to add value at all times.

Consider starting your own Group on LinkedIn. This is a powerful way to generate leads, though is time consuming and should be seen as a long-term strategy.

Many LinkedIn users think that searching for ideal clients, reaching out and connecting should be high on the priority list of daily activities. It can be but is not generally as effective as the five key activities described in this book. The tactics we have highlighted throughout are intended to draw these people *to you*, rather than you going to them - making it much easier to strike up conversations with them.

Compliance

It's worth spending a moment talking about compliance. This is not an exhaustive chapter on how financial advisers should use social media compliantly, but some general points need to be made.

For the avoidance of doubt, I am not a compliance officer, so you will always need to work with your own compliance team for definitive guidance.

However, I have met and worked with thousands of financial advisers, some of whom are heavy internet marketing and social media users and who between them have posted tens of thousands of tweets, articles, blogs, podcasts, videos and status updates with little, if any intervention from their compliance people.

I am conscious though, that different financial adviser firms have quite different approaches to compliance, with some not allowing their IFAs and advisers to even tweet about football results, right through to those who barely look at any social media posts throughout the year.

There isn't a right or wrong way to handle this topic, but we seem to be getting to a point where the most forward-thinking compliance teams allow advisers to post pretty well whatever they wish on social media within certain ground rules, and with random sample checks taking place once a quarter or every six months.

Those ground rules tend to be:

1. Do not post financial promotions on LinkedIn and social media
2. Do not give financial advice on social media
3. Do not bring the business into disrepute on social media
4. Be mindful of privacy issues
5. Stick within the confines of your company social media policy

Let's look at the first three:

Do not post financial promotions

In fact, you *can* post financial promotions on social media – as long as they go through your normal compliance process. But just don't, because no-one wants to see them in their social media feeds anyway. All they do is to reinforce the old perceptions that financial advisers are little more than salespeople.

I would also avoid adding "Contact me now" type remarks after posting a generic piece of value. For example, here is a real post that a financial adviser put on LinkedIn recently:

"The Chancellor was generous today as needed. At some point down the road taxes will increase and reliefs reduced. Personal wealth like Pensions and ISAs will be looked at.

If you need any help or advice on your options now in financial planning, I am happy to advise at [ABC Financial Planning].

The first paragraph is fine, but the second paragraph is unnecessary and clumsy.

Do not give financial advice on LinkedIn and social media

This is a no-brainer; just don't do it. But generic financial *education* is a quite different thing, and in many ways is the backbone of great content posted by many of the most successful financial advisers who use social media.

Do not bring the business into disrepute

We have all seen how easy it is for some people to get into arguments on social media, regardless of the topic being discussed. It is not pretty and can do untold damage to a financial advice business, so keep it professional.

Speaking of keeping it professional, I would like to add one further ground rule based on my own observations of many financial advisers' use of social media over the last fifteen years:

Do not bring the wider *profession* into disrepute

I have been working with financial advisers and their use of social media since 2004, and whilst the majority are very professional in their use of it, there is still a sizeable group of financial advisers whose use of online communications is anything but.

I am consistently shocked at how rude and discourteous some advisers are to each other online, and who have no room or respect for other advisers' views and business models.

Many of these comments are made in open forums, on blog posts, twitter and on news websites and do absolutely nothing to enhance the perception of the profession to the outside world.

Only a couple of days ago I saw an adviser in an online forum ask what one thing the profession needed to do to make itself more appealing to consumers. There were some great answers, all of which were perfectly valid (better marketing, consumer education etc.), but if I was to pick one thing, I would politely suggest that some advisers should think carefully about how they personally portray the profession to the outside world when engaging with their peers.

Daily Planner and Journal

What follows is approximately three months' worth of LinkedIn journaling. Use the space provided any way that you wish – either to plan your activity for a given week or to journal what you have done each day.

There are no hard and fast rules, but the idea is to get you into the habit of using LinkedIn in a clear and strategic way **each day**, because that is what gets results!

Remember, these are the Golden Five areas of activity that financial advisers should focus on when using LinkedIn to attract attention and to start conversations that will lead to new enquiries:

1. Check profile visits and engage with people
2. Post status updates that get attention
3. Comment on other people's content
4. Comment on content around followed hashtags
5. Post Company Status Updates

Very often you will find that people respond to your activity a few days afterwards, so use your journal to note any wins, observations or thoughts.

Important:

Before you start your activity, make a note of the number of profile visits that you are currently receiving, then monitor each week.

Also, every Monday you should check your other LinkedIn stats such as:

- Number of article views
- Number of appearances in search results
- Where your searchers work
- What your searchers do
- Keywords your searchers used

You should also do the same thing for your Company Page where you can see data on:

- Unique visitors
- Total follower count
- New followers
- Location of followers
- Post impressions
- Button clicks
- Comparisons to businesses that are similar to your own

Getting this data takes literally seconds, and it is really important that you get into the habit of checking your numbers both for your personal profile and your Company Page, because after a while you will start to see patterns in how the LinkedIn community responds to your activity. You can then adjust your activity and content so that you can maximise profile visits. I.e. do more of what works for you.

All of the Golden Five daily activities can be achieved in just ten minutes each day, though clearly there are going to be days when it takes longer or indeed shorter.

Ideally you should complete all five activities, but don't beat yourself up if you can only manage one or two. The point is that you get into the habit of some **daily** and **consistent** activity – and activities that are proven to lead to the best results – more profile views.

Once you are getting the profile views, it is over to you to get into conversations with people – just as you would if you were meeting a lead or prospect face to face. Remember – people buy people.

Don't forget to mix up the times of day that you are active on LinkedIn – again monitor your numbers to see what works best for you. And of course, if you are really keen, you can be active several times a day.

For **Y/N/P** on the coming pages, circle **Y**es, **N**o or **P**artially for whether or not you completed your LinkedIn activity that day.

Got a question?

Join our group at www.financialadvice.marketing and we will help you out. Alternatively, send me an email directly to philip@financialadvice.marketing.

Good luck!

GOLDEN FIVE LINKEDIN ACTIVITY   Date:

Check profile visits and engage with people   Y/N/P

Observations:

Post status updates   Y/N/P

If yes, what did you write about?

Comment on other people's content   Y/N/P

Observations:

Comment on content around followed hashtags   Y/N/P

Which hashtags?

Post Company Status Updates   Y/N/P

If yes, what did you write about?

Any other observations, quick wins or comments:

_____
_____
_____
_____

GOLDEN FIVE LINKEDIN ACTIVITY   **Date:**

Check profile visits and engage with people   Y/N/P

Observations:

Post status updates   Y/N/P

If yes, what did you write about?

Comment on other people's content   Y/N/P

Observations:

Comment on content around followed hashtags   Y/N/P

Which hashtags?

Post Company Status Updates   Y/N/P

If yes, what did you write about?

Any other observations, quick wins or comments:

_____
_____
_____
_____

GOLDEN FIVE LINKEDIN ACTIVITY Date:

Check profile visits and engage with people Y/N/P

Observations:

Post status updates Y/N/P

If yes, what did you write about?

Comment on other people's content Y/N/P

Observations:

Comment on content around followed hashtags Y/N/P

Which hashtags?

Post Company Status Updates Y/N/P

If yes, what did you write about?

Any other observations, quick wins or comments:

_____
_____
_____
_____

GOLDEN FIVE LINKEDIN ACTIVITY   **Date:**

Check profile visits and engage with people   Y/N/P

Observations:

Post status updates   Y/N/P

If yes, what did you write about?

Comment on other people's content   Y/N/P

Observations:

Comment on content around followed hashtags   Y/N/P

Which hashtags?

Post Company Status Updates   Y/N/P

If yes, what did you write about?

Any other observations, quick wins or comments:

_____
_____
_____
_____

GOLDEN FIVE LINKEDIN ACTIVITY   Date:

Check profile visits and engage with people   Y/N/P

Observations:

Post status updates   Y/N/P

If yes, what did you write about?

Comment on other people's content   Y/N/P

Observations:

Comment on content around followed hashtags   Y/N/P

Which hashtags?

Post Company Status Updates   Y/N/P

If yes, what did you write about?

Any other observations, quick wins or comments:

_____
_____
_____
_____

GOLDEN FIVE LINKEDIN ACTIVITY**Date:**

Check profile visits and engage with people**Y/N/P**

Observations:

Post status updates**Y/N/P**

If yes, what did you write about?

Comment on other people's content**Y/N/P**

Observations:

Comment on content around followed hashtags**Y/N/P**

Which hashtags?

Post Company Status Updates**Y/N/P**

If yes, what did you write about?

Any other observations, quick wins or comments:

_____
_____
_____
_____

GOLDEN FIVE LINKEDIN ACTIVITY   Date:

Check profile visits and engage with people   Y/N/P

Observations:

Post status updates   Y/N/P

If yes, what did you write about?

Comment on other people's content   Y/N/P

Observations:

Comment on content around followed hashtags   Y/N/P

Which hashtags?

Post Company Status Updates   Y/N/P

If yes, what did you write about?

Any other observations, quick wins or comments:

_____
_____
_____
_____

GOLDEN FIVE LINKEDIN ACTIVITY   **Date:**

Check profile visits and engage with people   Y/N/P

Observations:

Post status updates   Y/N/P

If yes, what did you write about?

Comment on other people's content   Y/N/P

Observations:

Comment on content around followed hashtags   Y/N/P

Which hashtags?

Post Company Status Updates   Y/N/P

If yes, what did you write about?

Any other observations, quick wins or comments:

_____
_____
_____
_____

GOLDEN FIVE LINKEDIN ACTIVITY   Date:

Check profile visits and engage with people   Y/N/P

Observations:

Post status updates   Y/N/P

If yes, what did you write about?

Comment on other people's content   Y/N/P

Observations:

Comment on content around followed hashtags   Y/N/P

Which hashtags?

Post Company Status Updates   Y/N/P

If yes, what did you write about?

Any other observations, quick wins or comments:

_____
_____
_____

GOLDEN FIVE LINKEDIN ACTIVITY   **Date:**

Check profile visits and engage with people   Y/N/P

Observations:

Post status updates   Y/N/P

If yes, what did you write about?

Comment on other people's content   Y/N/P

Observations:

Comment on content around followed hashtags   Y/N/P

Which hashtags?

Post Company Status Updates   Y/N/P

If yes, what did you write about?

Any other observations, quick wins or comments:

_____
_____
_____
_____

GOLDEN FIVE LINKEDIN ACTIVITY   Date:

Check profile visits and engage with people   Y/N/P

Observations:

Post status updates   Y/N/P

If yes, what did you write about?

Comment on other people's content   Y/N/P

Observations:

Comment on content around followed hashtags   Y/N/P

Which hashtags?

Post Company Status Updates   Y/N/P

If yes, what did you write about?

Any other observations, quick wins or comments:

_____
_____
_____
_____

GOLDEN FIVE LINKEDIN ACTIVITY   **Date:**

Check profile visits and engage with people   Y/N/P

Observations:

Post status updates   Y/N/P

If yes, what did you write about?

Comment on other people's content   Y/N/P

Observations:

Comment on content around followed hashtags   Y/N/P

Which hashtags?

Post Company Status Updates   Y/N/P

If yes, what did you write about?

Any other observations, quick wins or comments:

_____
_____
_____
_____

GOLDEN FIVE LINKEDIN ACTIVITY   Date:

Check profile visits and engage with people   Y/N/P

Observations:

Post status updates   Y/N/P

If yes, what did you write about?

Comment on other people's content   Y/N/P

Observations:

Comment on content around followed hashtags   Y/N/P

Which hashtags?

Post Company Status Updates   Y/N/P

If yes, what did you write about?

Any other observations, quick wins or comments:

_____
_____
_____
_____

GOLDEN FIVE LINKEDIN ACTIVITY   **Date:**

Check profile visits and engage with people   Y/N/P

Observations:

Post status updates   Y/N/P

If yes, what did you write about?

Comment on other people's content   Y/N/P

Observations:

Comment on content around followed hashtags   Y/N/P

Which hashtags?

Post Company Status Updates   Y/N/P

If yes, what did you write about?

Any other observations, quick wins or comments:

_____
_____
_____
_____

GOLDEN FIVE LINKEDIN ACTIVITY   Date:

Check profile visits and engage with people   Y/N/P

Observations:

Post status updates   Y/N/P

If yes, what did you write about?

Comment on other people's content   Y/N/P

Observations:

Comment on content around followed hashtags   Y/N/P

Which hashtags?

Post Company Status Updates   Y/N/P

If yes, what did you write about?

Any other observations, quick wins or comments:

_____
_____
_____
_____

GOLDEN FIVE LINKEDIN ACTIVITY   Date:

Check profile visits and engage with people   Y/N/P

Observations:

Post status updates   Y/N/P

If yes, what did you write about?

Comment on other people's content   Y/N/P

Observations:

Comment on content around followed hashtags   Y/N/P

Which hashtags?

Post Company Status Updates   Y/N/P

If yes, what did you write about?

Any other observations, quick wins or comments:

_____
_____
_____
_____

GOLDEN FIVE LINKEDIN ACTIVITY   Date:

Check profile visits and engage with people   Y/N/P

Observations:

Post status updates   Y/N/P

If yes, what did you write about?

Comment on other people's content   Y/N/P

Observations:

Comment on content around followed hashtags   Y/N/P

Which hashtags?

Post Company Status Updates   Y/N/P

If yes, what did you write about?

Any other observations, quick wins or comments:

_____
_____
_____
_____

GOLDEN FIVE LINKEDIN ACTIVITY   Date:

Check profile visits and engage with people   Y/N/P

Observations:

Post status updates   Y/N/P

If yes, what did you write about?

Comment on other people's content   Y/N/P

Observations:

Comment on content around followed hashtags   Y/N/P

Which hashtags?

Post Company Status Updates   Y/N/P

If yes, what did you write about?

Any other observations, quick wins or comments:

_____
_____
_____
_____

GOLDEN FIVE LINKEDIN ACTIVITY   Date:

Check profile visits and engage with people   Y/N/P

Observations:

Post status updates   Y/N/P

If yes, what did you write about?

Comment on other people's content   Y/N/P

Observations:

Comment on content around followed hashtags   Y/N/P

Which hashtags?

Post Company Status Updates   Y/N/P

If yes, what did you write about?

Any other observations, quick wins or comments:

_____
_____
_____
_____

GOLDEN FIVE LINKEDIN ACTIVITY   **Date:**

Check profile visits and engage with people   Y/N/P

Observations:

Post status updates   Y/N/P

If yes, what did you write about?

Comment on other people's content   Y/N/P

Observations:

Comment on content around followed hashtags   Y/N/P

Which hashtags?

Post Company Status Updates   Y/N/P

If yes, what did you write about?

Any other observations, quick wins or comments:

_____
_____
_____
_____

GOLDEN FIVE LINKEDIN ACTIVITY Date:

Check profile visits and engage with people Y/N/P

Observations:

Post status updates Y/N/P

If yes, what did you write about?

Comment on other people's content Y/N/P

Observations:

Comment on content around followed hashtags Y/N/P

Which hashtags?

Post Company Status Updates Y/N/P

If yes, what did you write about?

Any other observations, quick wins or comments:

_____
_____
_____
_____

GOLDEN FIVE LINKEDIN ACTIVITY   **Date:**

Check profile visits and engage with people   Y/N/P

Observations:

Post status updates   Y/N/P

If yes, what did you write about?

Comment on other people's content   Y/N/P

Observations:

Comment on content around followed hashtags   Y/N/P

Which hashtags?

Post Company Status Updates   Y/N/P

If yes, what did you write about?

Any other observations, quick wins or comments:

_____
_____
_____
_____

GOLDEN FIVE LINKEDIN ACTIVITY   Date:

Check profile visits and engage with people   Y/N/P

Observations:

Post status updates   Y/N/P

If yes, what did you write about?

Comment on other people's content   Y/N/P

Observations:

Comment on content around followed hashtags   Y/N/P

Which hashtags?

Post Company Status Updates   Y/N/P

If yes, what did you write about?

Any other observations, quick wins or comments:

_____
_____
_____
_____

GOLDEN FIVE LINKEDIN ACTIVITY   Date:

Check profile visits and engage with people   Y/N/P

Observations:

Post status updates   Y/N/P

If yes, what did you write about?

Comment on other people's content   Y/N/P

Observations:

Comment on content around followed hashtags   Y/N/P

Which hashtags?

Post Company Status Updates   Y/N/P

If yes, what did you write about?

Any other observations, quick wins or comments:

_____
_____
_____
_____

GOLDEN FIVE LINKEDIN ACTIVITY   Date:

Check profile visits and engage with people   Y/N/P

Observations:

Post status updates   Y/N/P

If yes, what did you write about?

Comment on other people's content   Y/N/P

Observations:

Comment on content around followed hashtags   Y/N/P

Which hashtags?

Post Company Status Updates   Y/N/P

If yes, what did you write about?

Any other observations, quick wins or comments:

_____
_____
_____
_____

GOLDEN FIVE LINKEDIN ACTIVITY   Date:

Check profile visits and engage with people   Y/N/P

Observations:

Post status updates   Y/N/P

If yes, what did you write about?

Comment on other people's content   Y/N/P

Observations:

Comment on content around followed hashtags   Y/N/P

Which hashtags?

Post Company Status Updates   Y/N/P

If yes, what did you write about?

Any other observations, quick wins or comments:

_____
_____
_____
_____

GOLDEN FIVE LINKEDIN ACTIVITY   Date:

Check profile visits and engage with people   Y/N/P

Observations:

Post status updates   Y/N/P

If yes, what did you write about?

Comment on other people's content   Y/N/P

Observations:

Comment on content around followed hashtags   Y/N/P

Which hashtags?

Post Company Status Updates   Y/N/P

If yes, what did you write about?

Any other observations, quick wins or comments:

_____
_____
_____
_____

GOLDEN FIVE LINKEDIN ACTIVITY   Date:

Check profile visits and engage with people   Y/N/P

Observations:

Post status updates   Y/N/P

If yes, what did you write about?

Comment on other people's content   Y/N/P

Observations:

Comment on content around followed hashtags   Y/N/P

Which hashtags?

Post Company Status Updates   Y/N/P

If yes, what did you write about?

Any other observations, quick wins or comments:

_____
_____
_____
_____

GOLDEN FIVE LINKEDIN ACTIVITY   Date:

Check profile visits and engage with people   Y/N/P

Observations:

Post status updates   Y/N/P

If yes, what did you write about?

Comment on other people's content   Y/N/P

Observations:

Comment on content around followed hashtags   Y/N/P

Which hashtags?

Post Company Status Updates   Y/N/P

If yes, what did you write about?

Any other observations, quick wins or comments:

_____
_____
_____
_____

GOLDEN FIVE LINKEDIN ACTIVITY   Date:

Check profile visits and engage with people   Y/N/P

Observations:

Post status updates   Y/N/P

If yes, what did you write about?

Comment on other people's content   Y/N/P

Observations:

Comment on content around followed hashtags   Y/N/P

Which hashtags?

Post Company Status Updates   Y/N/P

If yes, what did you write about?

Any other observations, quick wins or comments:

_____
_____
_____
_____

GOLDEN FIVE LINKEDIN ACTIVITY   Date:

Check profile visits and engage with people   Y/N/P

Observations:

Post status updates   Y/N/P

If yes, what did you write about?

Comment on other people's content   Y/N/P

Observations:

Comment on content around followed hashtags   Y/N/P

Which hashtags?

Post Company Status Updates   Y/N/P

If yes, what did you write about?

Any other observations, quick wins or comments:

_____
_____
_____

GOLDEN FIVE LINKEDIN ACTIVITY   **Date:**

Check profile visits and engage with people   Y/N/P

Observations:

Post status updates   Y/N/P

If yes, what did you write about?

Comment on other people's content   Y/N/P

Observations:

Comment on content around followed hashtags   Y/N/P

Which hashtags?

Post Company Status Updates   Y/N/P

If yes, what did you write about?

Any other observations, quick wins or comments:

_____
_____
_____
_____

GOLDEN FIVE LINKEDIN ACTIVITY　　　　**Date:**

Check profile visits and engage with people　　　Y/N/P

Observations:

Post status updates　　　Y/N/P

If yes, what did you write about?

Comment on other people's content　　　Y/N/P

Observations:

Comment on content around followed hashtags　　　Y/N/P

Which hashtags?

Post Company Status Updates　　　Y/N/P

If yes, what did you write about?

Any other observations, quick wins or comments:

_____
_____
_____
_____

GOLDEN FIVE LINKEDIN ACTIVITY   **Date:**

Check profile visits and engage with people   Y/N/P

Observations:

Post status updates   Y/N/P

If yes, what did you write about?

Comment on other people's content   Y/N/P

Observations:

Comment on content around followed hashtags Y/N/P

Which hashtags?

Post Company Status Updates   Y/N/P

If yes, what did you write about?

Any other observations, quick wins or comments:

_____
_____
_____
_____

GOLDEN FIVE LINKEDIN ACTIVITY   **Date:**

Check profile visits and engage with people   Y/N/P

Observations:

Post status updates   Y/N/P

If yes, what did you write about?

Comment on other people's content   Y/N/P

Observations:

Comment on content around followed hashtags   Y/N/P

Which hashtags?

Post Company Status Updates   Y/N/P

If yes, what did you write about?

Any other observations, quick wins or comments:

_____
_____
_____
_____

GOLDEN FIVE LINKEDIN ACTIVITY   Date:

Check profile visits and engage with people   Y/N/P

Observations:

Post status updates   Y/N/P

If yes, what did you write about?

Comment on other people's content   Y/N/P

Observations:

Comment on content around followed hashtags   Y/N/P

Which hashtags?

Post Company Status Updates   Y/N/P

If yes, what did you write about?

Any other observations, quick wins or comments:

_____
_____
_____
_____

GOLDEN FIVE LINKEDIN ACTIVITY   Date:

Check profile visits and engage with people   Y/N/P

Observations:

Post status updates   Y/N/P

If yes, what did you write about?

Comment on other people's content   Y/N/P

Observations:

Comment on content around followed hashtags   Y/N/P

Which hashtags?

Post Company Status Updates   Y/N/P

If yes, what did you write about?

Any other observations, quick wins or comments:

_____
_____
_____
_____

GOLDEN FIVE LINKEDIN ACTIVITY   Date:

Check profile visits and engage with people   Y/N/P

Observations:

Post status updates   Y/N/P

If yes, what did you write about?

Comment on other people's content   Y/N/P

Observations:

Comment on content around followed hashtags   Y/N/P

Which hashtags?

Post Company Status Updates   Y/N/P

If yes, what did you write about?

Any other observations, quick wins or comments:

_____
_____
_____
_____

GOLDEN FIVE LINKEDIN ACTIVITY   Date:

Check profile visits and engage with people   Y/N/P

Observations:

Post status updates   Y/N/P

If yes, what did you write about?

Comment on other people's content   Y/N/P

Observations:

Comment on content around followed hashtags   Y/N/P

Which hashtags?

Post Company Status Updates   Y/N/P

If yes, what did you write about?

Any other observations, quick wins or comments:

_____
_____
_____
_____

GOLDEN FIVE LINKEDIN ACTIVITY   Date:

Check profile visits and engage with people   Y/N/P

Observations:

Post status updates   Y/N/P

If yes, what did you write about?

Comment on other people's content   Y/N/P

Observations:

Comment on content around followed hashtags   Y/N/P

Which hashtags?

Post Company Status Updates   Y/N/P

If yes, what did you write about?

Any other observations, quick wins or comments:

_____
_____
_____
_____

GOLDEN FIVE LINKEDIN ACTIVITY   **Date:**

Check profile visits and engage with people   Y/N/P

Observations:

Post status updates   Y/N/P

If yes, what did you write about?

Comment on other people's content   Y/N/P

Observations:

Comment on content around followed hashtags   Y/N/P

Which hashtags?

Post Company Status Updates   Y/N/P

If yes, what did you write about?

Any other observations, quick wins or comments:

_____
_____
_____
_____

GOLDEN FIVE LINKEDIN ACTIVITY   Date:

Check profile visits and engage with people   Y/N/P

Observations:

Post status updates   Y/N/P

If yes, what did you write about?

Comment on other people's content   Y/N/P

Observations:

Comment on content around followed hashtags   Y/N/P

Which hashtags?

Post Company Status Updates   Y/N/P

If yes, what did you write about?

Any other observations, quick wins or comments:

_____
_____
_____
_____

GOLDEN FIVE LINKEDIN ACTIVITY   Date:

Check profile visits and engage with people   Y/N/P

Observations:

Post status updates   Y/N/P

If yes, what did you write about?

Comment on other people's content   Y/N/P

Observations:

Comment on content around followed hashtags   Y/N/P

Which hashtags?

Post Company Status Updates   Y/N/P

If yes, what did you write about?

Any other observations, quick wins or comments:

_____
_____
_____
_____

GOLDEN FIVE LINKEDIN ACTIVITY   Date:

Check profile visits and engage with people   Y/N/P

Observations:

Post status updates   Y/N/P

If yes, what did you write about?

Comment on other people's content   Y/N/P

Observations:

Comment on content around followed hashtags   Y/N/P

Which hashtags?

Post Company Status Updates   Y/N/P

If yes, what did you write about?

Any other observations, quick wins or comments:

_____
_____
_____
_____

GOLDEN FIVE LINKEDIN ACTIVITY   Date:

Check profile visits and engage with people   Y/N/P

Observations:

Post status updates   Y/N/P

If yes, what did you write about?

Comment on other people's content   Y/N/P

Observations:

Comment on content around followed hashtags   Y/N/P

Which hashtags?

Post Company Status Updates   Y/N/P

If yes, what did you write about?

Any other observations, quick wins or comments:

_____
_____
_____
_____

GOLDEN FIVE LINKEDIN ACTIVITY   **Date:**

Check profile visits and engage with people   Y/N/P

Observations:

Post status updates   Y/N/P

If yes, what did you write about?

Comment on other people's content   Y/N/P

Observations:

Comment on content around followed hashtags   Y/N/P

Which hashtags?

Post Company Status Updates   Y/N/P

If yes, what did you write about?

Any other observations, quick wins or comments:

_____
_____
_____
_____

GOLDEN FIVE LINKEDIN ACTIVITY   Date:

Check profile visits and engage with people   Y/N/P

Observations:

Post status updates   Y/N/P

If yes, what did you write about?

Comment on other people's content   Y/N/P

Observations:

Comment on content around followed hashtags   Y/N/P

Which hashtags?

Post Company Status Updates   Y/N/P

If yes, what did you write about?

Any other observations, quick wins or comments:

_____
_____
_____
_____

GOLDEN FIVE LINKEDIN ACTIVITY   Date:

Check profile visits and engage with people   Y/N/P

Observations:

Post status updates   Y/N/P

If yes, what did you write about?

Comment on other people's content   Y/N/P

Observations:

Comment on content around followed hashtags   Y/N/P

Which hashtags?

Post Company Status Updates   Y/N/P

If yes, what did you write about?

Any other observations, quick wins or comments:

_____
_____
_____
_____

GOLDEN FIVE LINKEDIN ACTIVITY   Date:

Check profile visits and engage with people   Y/N/P

Observations:

Post status updates   Y/N/P

If yes, what did you write about?

Comment on other people's content   Y/N/P

Observations:

Comment on content around followed hashtags   Y/N/P

Which hashtags?

Post Company Status Updates   Y/N/P

If yes, what did you write about?

Any other observations, quick wins or comments:

_____
_____
_____
_____

GOLDEN FIVE LINKEDIN ACTIVITY   **Date:**

Check profile visits and engage with people   Y/N/P

Observations:

Post status updates   Y/N/P

If yes, what did you write about?

Comment on other people's content   Y/N/P

Observations:

Comment on content around followed hashtags   Y/N/P

Which hashtags?

Post Company Status Updates   Y/N/P

If yes, what did you write about?

Any other observations, quick wins or comments:

_____
_____
_____
_____

GOLDEN FIVE LINKEDIN ACTIVITY   Date:

Check profile visits and engage with people   Y/N/P

Observations:

Post status updates   Y/N/P

If yes, what did you write about?

Comment on other people's content   Y/N/P

Observations:

Comment on content around followed hashtags   Y/N/P

Which hashtags?

Post Company Status Updates   Y/N/P

If yes, what did you write about?

Any other observations, quick wins or comments:

_____
_____
_____
_____

GOLDEN FIVE LINKEDIN ACTIVITY   **Date:**

Check profile visits and engage with people   Y/N/P

Observations:

Post status updates   Y/N/P

If yes, what did you write about?

Comment on other people's content   Y/N/P

Observations:

Comment on content around followed hashtags   Y/N/P

Which hashtags?

Post Company Status Updates   Y/N/P

If yes, what did you write about?

Any other observations, quick wins or comments:

_____
_____
_____
_____

GOLDEN FIVE LINKEDIN ACTIVITY   **Date:**

Check profile visits and engage with people   Y/N/P

Observations:

Post status updates   Y/N/P

If yes, what did you write about?

Comment on other people's content   Y/N/P

Observations:

Comment on content around followed hashtags   Y/N/P

Which hashtags?

Post Company Status Updates   Y/N/P

If yes, what did you write about?

Any other observations, quick wins or comments:

_____
_____
_____

GOLDEN FIVE LINKEDIN ACTIVITY   Date:

Check profile visits and engage with people   Y/N/P

Observations:

Post status updates   Y/N/P

If yes, what did you write about?

Comment on other people's content   Y/N/P

Observations:

Comment on content around followed hashtags   Y/N/P

Which hashtags?

Post Company Status Updates   Y/N/P

If yes, what did you write about?

Any other observations, quick wins or comments:

_____
_____
_____
_____

GOLDEN FIVE LINKEDIN ACTIVITY   Date:

Check profile visits and engage with people   Y/N/P

Observations:

Post status updates   Y/N/P

If yes, what did you write about?

Comment on other people's content   Y/N/P

Observations:

Comment on content around followed hashtags   Y/N/P

Which hashtags?

Post Company Status Updates   Y/N/P

If yes, what did you write about?

Any other observations, quick wins or comments:

_____
_____
_____
_____

GOLDEN FIVE LINKEDIN ACTIVITY   Date:

Check profile visits and engage with people   Y/N/P

Observations:

Post status updates   Y/N/P

If yes, what did you write about?

Comment on other people's content   Y/N/P

Observations:

Comment on content around followed hashtags   Y/N/P

Which hashtags?

Post Company Status Updates   Y/N/P

If yes, what did you write about?

Any other observations, quick wins or comments:

_____
_____
_____
_____

GOLDEN FIVE LINKEDIN ACTIVITY   Date:

Check profile visits and engage with people   Y/N/P

Observations:

Post status updates   Y/N/P

If yes, what did you write about?

Comment on other people's content   Y/N/P

Observations:

Comment on content around followed hashtags   Y/N/P

Which hashtags?

Post Company Status Updates   Y/N/P

If yes, what did you write about?

Any other observations, quick wins or comments:

_____
_____
_____
_____

GOLDEN FIVE LINKEDIN ACTIVITY   **Date:**

Check profile visits and engage with people   Y/N/P

Observations:

Post status updates   Y/N/P

If yes, what did you write about?

Comment on other people's content   Y/N/P

Observations:

Comment on content around followed hashtags   Y/N/P

Which hashtags?

Post Company Status Updates   Y/N/P

If yes, what did you write about?

Any other observations, quick wins or comments:

_____
_____
_____
_____

GOLDEN FIVE LINKEDIN ACTIVITY   Date:

Check profile visits and engage with people   Y/N/P

Observations:

Post status updates   Y/N/P

If yes, what did you write about?

Comment on other people's content   Y/N/P

Observations:

Comment on content around followed hashtags   Y/N/P

Which hashtags?

Post Company Status Updates   Y/N/P

If yes, what did you write about?

Any other observations, quick wins or comments:

_____
_____
_____
_____

GOLDEN FIVE LINKEDIN ACTIVITY   **Date:**

Check profile visits and engage with people   Y/N/P

Observations:

Post status updates   Y/N/P

If yes, what did you write about?

Comment on other people's content   Y/N/P

Observations:

Comment on content around followed hashtags   Y/N/P

Which hashtags?

Post Company Status Updates   Y/N/P

If yes, what did you write about?

Any other observations, quick wins or comments:

_____
_____
_____
_____

GOLDEN FIVE LINKEDIN ACTIVITY   Date:

Check profile visits and engage with people   Y/N/P

Observations:

Post status updates   Y/N/P

If yes, what did you write about?

Comment on other people's content   Y/N/P

Observations:

Comment on content around followed hashtags   Y/N/P

Which hashtags?

Post Company Status Updates   Y/N/P

If yes, what did you write about?

Any other observations, quick wins or comments:

_____
_____
_____
_____

GOLDEN FIVE LINKEDIN ACTIVITY   Date:

Check profile visits and engage with people   Y/N/P

Observations:

Post status updates   Y/N/P

If yes, what did you write about?

Comment on other people's content   Y/N/P

Observations:

Comment on content around followed hashtags   Y/N/P

Which hashtags?

Post Company Status Updates   Y/N/P

If yes, what did you write about?

Any other observations, quick wins or comments:

_____
_____
_____
_____

GOLDEN FIVE LINKEDIN ACTIVITY   Date:

Check profile visits and engage with people   Y/N/P

Observations:

Post status updates   Y/N/P

If yes, what did you write about?

Comment on other people's content   Y/N/P

Observations:

Comment on content around followed hashtags   Y/N/P

Which hashtags?

Post Company Status Updates   Y/N/P

If yes, what did you write about?

Any other observations, quick wins or comments:

_____
_____
_____
_____

GOLDEN FIVE LINKEDIN ACTIVITY**Date:**

Check profile visits and engage with people   Y/N/P

Observations:

Post status updates   Y/N/P

If yes, what did you write about?

Comment on other people's content   Y/N/P

Observations:

Comment on content around followed hashtags   Y/N/P

Which hashtags?

Post Company Status Updates   Y/N/P

If yes, what did you write about?

Any other observations, quick wins or comments:

_____
_____
_____
_____

GOLDEN FIVE LINKEDIN ACTIVITY   Date:

Check profile visits and engage with people   Y/N/P

Observations:

Post status updates   Y/N/P

If yes, what did you write about?

Comment on other people's content   Y/N/P

Observations:

Comment on content around followed hashtags   Y/N/P

Which hashtags?

Post Company Status Updates   Y/N/P

If yes, what did you write about?

Any other observations, quick wins or comments:

_____
_____
_____
_____

GOLDEN FIVE LINKEDIN ACTIVITY   **Date:**

Check profile visits and engage with people   Y/N/P

Observations:

Post status updates   Y/N/P

If yes, what did you write about?

Comment on other people's content   Y/N/P

Observations:

Comment on content around followed hashtags   Y/N/P

Which hashtags?

Post Company Status Updates   Y/N/P

If yes, what did you write about?

Any other observations, quick wins or comments:

_____
_____
_____
_____

GOLDEN FIVE LINKEDIN ACTIVITY   Date:

Check profile visits and engage with people   Y/N/P

Observations:

Post status updates   Y/N/P

If yes, what did you write about?

Comment on other people's content   Y/N/P

Observations:

Comment on content around followed hashtags   Y/N/P

Which hashtags?

Post Company Status Updates   Y/N/P

If yes, what did you write about?

Any other observations, quick wins or comments:

_____
_____
_____
_____

GOLDEN FIVE LINKEDIN ACTIVITY   Date:

Check profile visits and engage with people   Y/N/P

Observations:

Post status updates   Y/N/P

If yes, what did you write about?

Comment on other people's content   Y/N/P

Observations:

Comment on content around followed hashtags   Y/N/P

Which hashtags?

Post Company Status Updates   Y/N/P

If yes, what did you write about?

Any other observations, quick wins or comments:

_____
_____
_____
_____

GOLDEN FIVE LINKEDIN ACTIVITY   Date:

Check profile visits and engage with people   Y/N/P

Observations:

Post status updates   Y/N/P

If yes, what did you write about?

Comment on other people's content   Y/N/P

Observations:

Comment on content around followed hashtags   Y/N/P

Which hashtags?

Post Company Status Updates   Y/N/P

If yes, what did you write about?

Any other observations, quick wins or comments:
_____
_____
_____
_____

GOLDEN FIVE LINKEDIN ACTIVITY   Date:

Check profile visits and engage with people   Y/N/P

Observations:

Post status updates   Y/N/P

If yes, what did you write about?

Comment on other people's content   Y/N/P

Observations:

Comment on content around followed hashtags   Y/N/P

Which hashtags?

Post Company Status Updates   Y/N/P

If yes, what did you write about?

Any other observations, quick wins or comments:

_____
_____
_____
_____

GOLDEN FIVE LINKEDIN ACTIVITY   Date:

Check profile visits and engage with people   Y/N/P

Observations:

Post status updates   Y/N/P

If yes, what did you write about?

Comment on other people's content   Y/N/P

Observations:

Comment on content around followed hashtags   Y/N/P

Which hashtags?

Post Company Status Updates   Y/N/P

If yes, what did you write about?

Any other observations, quick wins or comments:

_____
_____
_____
_____

GOLDEN FIVE LINKEDIN ACTIVITY   Date:

Check profile visits and engage with people   Y/N/P

Observations:

Post status updates   Y/N/P

If yes, what did you write about?

Comment on other people's content   Y/N/P

Observations:

Comment on content around followed hashtags   Y/N/P

Which hashtags?

Post Company Status Updates   Y/N/P

If yes, what did you write about?

Any other observations, quick wins or comments:

_____
_____
_____
_____

GOLDEN FIVE LINKEDIN ACTIVITY   Date:

Check profile visits and engage with people   Y/N/P

Observations:

Post status updates   Y/N/P

If yes, what did you write about?

Comment on other people's content   Y/N/P

Observations:

Comment on content around followed hashtags   Y/N/P

Which hashtags?

Post Company Status Updates   Y/N/P

If yes, what did you write about?

Any other observations, quick wins or comments:

_____
_____
_____
_____

GOLDEN FIVE LINKEDIN ACTIVITY   Date:

Check profile visits and engage with people   Y/N/P

Observations:

Post status updates   Y/N/P

If yes, what did you write about?

Comment on other people's content   Y/N/P

Observations:

Comment on content around followed hashtags   Y/N/P

Which hashtags?

Post Company Status Updates   Y/N/P

If yes, what did you write about?

Any other observations, quick wins or comments:

_____
_____
_____
_____

GOLDEN FIVE LINKEDIN ACTIVITY Date:

Check profile visits and engage with people Y/N/P

Observations:

Post status updates Y/N/P

If yes, what did you write about?

Comment on other people's content Y/N/P

Observations:

Comment on content around followed hashtags Y/N/P

Which hashtags?

Post Company Status Updates Y/N/P

If yes, what did you write about?

Any other observations, quick wins or comments:

_____
_____
_____
_____

GOLDEN FIVE LINKEDIN ACTIVITY   **Date:**

Check profile visits and engage with people   Y/N/P

Observations:

Post status updates   Y/N/P

If yes, what did you write about?

Comment on other people's content   Y/N/P

Observations:

Comment on content around followed hashtags   Y/N/P

Which hashtags?

Post Company Status Updates   Y/N/P

If yes, what did you write about?

Any other observations, quick wins or comments:

_____
_____
_____
_____

GOLDEN FIVE LINKEDIN ACTIVITY   Date:

Check profile visits and engage with people   Y/N/P

Observations:

Post status updates   Y/N/P

If yes, what did you write about?

Comment on other people's content   Y/N/P

Observations:

Comment on content around followed hashtags   Y/N/P

Which hashtags?

Post Company Status Updates   Y/N/P

If yes, what did you write about?

Any other observations, quick wins or comments:

_____
_____
_____
_____

GOLDEN FIVE LINKEDIN ACTIVITY   Date:

Check profile visits and engage with people   Y/N/P

Observations:

Post status updates   Y/N/P

If yes, what did you write about?

Comment on other people's content   Y/N/P

Observations:

Comment on content around followed hashtags   Y/N/P

Which hashtags?

Post Company Status Updates   Y/N/P

If yes, what did you write about?

Any other observations, quick wins or comments:

_____
_____
_____
_____

GOLDEN FIVE LINKEDIN ACTIVITY   Date:

Check profile visits and engage with people   Y/N/P

Observations:

Post status updates   Y/N/P

If yes, what did you write about?

Comment on other people's content   Y/N/P

Observations:

Comment on content around followed hashtags   Y/N/P

Which hashtags?

Post Company Status Updates   Y/N/P

If yes, what did you write about?

Any other observations, quick wins or comments:

_____
_____
_____

GOLDEN FIVE LINKEDIN ACTIVITY   **Date:**

Check profile visits and engage with people   Y/N/P

Observations:

Post status updates   Y/N/P

If yes, what did you write about?

Comment on other people's content   Y/N/P

Observations:

Comment on content around followed hashtags   Y/N/P

Which hashtags?

Post Company Status Updates   Y/N/P

If yes, what did you write about?

Any other observations, quick wins or comments:

_____
_____
_____
_____

GOLDEN FIVE LINKEDIN ACTIVITY   Date:

Check profile visits and engage with people   Y/N/P

Observations:

Post status updates   Y/N/P

If yes, what did you write about?

Comment on other people's content   Y/N/P

Observations:

Comment on content around followed hashtags   Y/N/P

Which hashtags?

Post Company Status Updates   Y/N/P

If yes, what did you write about?

Any other observations, quick wins or comments:

_____
_____
_____
_____

GOLDEN FIVE LINKEDIN ACTIVITY   Date:

Check profile visits and engage with people   Y/N/P

Observations:

Post status updates   Y/N/P

If yes, what did you write about?

Comment on other people's content   Y/N/P

Observations:

Comment on content around followed hashtags   Y/N/P

Which hashtags?

Post Company Status Updates   Y/N/P

If yes, what did you write about?

Any other observations, quick wins or comments:

_____
_____
_____
_____

GOLDEN FIVE LINKEDIN ACTIVITY   Date:

Check profile visits and engage with people   Y/N/P

Observations:

Post status updates   Y/N/P

If yes, what did you write about?

Comment on other people's content   Y/N/P

Observations:

Comment on content around followed hashtags   Y/N/P

Which hashtags?

Post Company Status Updates   Y/N/P

If yes, what did you write about?

Any other observations, quick wins or comments:

_____
_____
_____
_____

GOLDEN FIVE LINKEDIN ACTIVITY   Date:

Check profile visits and engage with people   Y/N/P

Observations:

Post status updates   Y/N/P

If yes, what did you write about?

Comment on other people's content   Y/N/P

Observations:

Comment on content around followed hashtags   Y/N/P

Which hashtags?

Post Company Status Updates   Y/N/P

If yes, what did you write about?

Any other observations, quick wins or comments:

_____
_____
_____
_____

GOLDEN FIVE LINKEDIN ACTIVITY   Date:

Check profile visits and engage with people   Y/N/P

Observations:

Post status updates   Y/N/P

If yes, what did you write about?

Comment on other people's content   Y/N/P

Observations:

Comment on content around followed hashtags   Y/N/P

Which hashtags?

Post Company Status Updates   Y/N/P

If yes, what did you write about?

Any other observations, quick wins or comments:

_____
_____
_____

GOLDEN FIVE LINKEDIN ACTIVITY   Date:

Check profile visits and engage with people   Y/N/P

Observations:

Post status updates   Y/N/P

If yes, what did you write about?

Comment on other people's content   Y/N/P

Observations:

Comment on content around followed hashtags   Y/N/P

Which hashtags?

Post Company Status Updates   Y/N/P

If yes, what did you write about?

Any other observations, quick wins or comments:

_____
_____
_____
_____

GOLDEN FIVE LINKEDIN ACTIVITY   Date:

Check profile visits and engage with people   Y/N/P

Observations:

Post status updates   Y/N/P

If yes, what did you write about?

Comment on other people's content   Y/N/P

Observations:

Comment on content around followed hashtags   Y/N/P

Which hashtags?

Post Company Status Updates   Y/N/P

If yes, what did you write about?

Any other observations, quick wins or comments:

_____
_____
_____
_____

GOLDEN FIVE LINKEDIN ACTIVITY   Date:

Check profile visits and engage with people   Y/N/P

Observations:

Post status updates   Y/N/P

If yes, what did you write about?

Comment on other people's content   Y/N/P

Observations:

Comment on content around followed hashtags   Y/N/P

Which hashtags?

Post Company Status Updates   Y/N/P

If yes, what did you write about?

Any other observations, quick wins or comments:

_____
_____
_____
_____

GOLDEN FIVE LINKEDIN ACTIVITY   Date:

Check profile visits and engage with people   Y/N/P

Observations:

Post status updates   Y/N/P

If yes, what did you write about?

Comment on other people's content   Y/N/P

Observations:

Comment on content around followed hashtags   Y/N/P

Which hashtags?

Post Company Status Updates   Y/N/P

If yes, what did you write about?

Any other observations, quick wins or comments:

_____
_____
_____
_____

GOLDEN FIVE LINKEDIN ACTIVITY   Date:

Check profile visits and engage with people   Y/N/P

Observations:

Post status updates   Y/N/P

If yes, what did you write about?

Comment on other people's content   Y/N/P

Observations:

Comment on content around followed hashtags   Y/N/P

Which hashtags?

Post Company Status Updates   Y/N/P

If yes, what did you write about?

Any other observations, quick wins or comments:

_____
_____
_____
_____

GOLDEN FIVE LINKEDIN ACTIVITY   Date:

Check profile visits and engage with people   Y/N/P

Observations:

Post status updates   Y/N/P

If yes, what did you write about?

Comment on other people's content   Y/N/P

Observations:

Comment on content around followed hashtags   Y/N/P

Which hashtags?

Post Company Status Updates   Y/N/P

If yes, what did you write about?

Any other observations, quick wins or comments:

_____
_____
_____
_____

GOLDEN FIVE LINKEDIN ACTIVITY   Date:

Check profile visits and engage with people   Y/N/P

Observations:

Post status updates   Y/N/P

If yes, what did you write about?

Comment on other people's content   Y/N/P

Observations:

Comment on content around followed hashtags   Y/N/P

Which hashtags?

Post Company Status Updates   Y/N/P

If yes, what did you write about?

Any other observations, quick wins or comments:

_____
_____
_____
_____

GOLDEN FIVE LINKEDIN ACTIVITY   Date:

Check profile visits and engage with people   Y/N/P

Observations:

Post status updates   Y/N/P

If yes, what did you write about?

Comment on other people's content   Y/N/P

Observations:

Comment on content around followed hashtags   Y/N/P

Which hashtags?

Post Company Status Updates   Y/N/P

If yes, what did you write about?

Any other observations, quick wins or comments:

_____
_____
_____
_____

GOLDEN FIVE LINKEDIN ACTIVITY   Date:

Check profile visits and engage with people   Y/N/P

Observations:

Post status updates   Y/N/P

If yes, what did you write about?

Comment on other people's content   Y/N/P

Observations:

Comment on content around followed hashtags   Y/N/P

Which hashtags?

Post Company Status Updates   Y/N/P

If yes, what did you write about?

Any other observations, quick wins or comments:

_____
_____
_____
_____

GOLDEN FIVE LINKEDIN ACTIVITY   Date:

Check profile visits and engage with people   Y/N/P

Observations:

Post status updates   Y/N/P

If yes, what did you write about?

Comment on other people's content   Y/N/P

Observations:

Comment on content around followed hashtags   Y/N/P

Which hashtags?

Post Company Status Updates   Y/N/P

If yes, what did you write about?

Any other observations, quick wins or comments:

_____
_____
_____
_____

GOLDEN FIVE LINKEDIN ACTIVITY   Date:

Check profile visits and engage with people   Y/N/P

Observations:

Post status updates   Y/N/P

If yes, what did you write about?

Comment on other people's content   Y/N/P

Observations:

Comment on content around followed hashtags   Y/N/P

Which hashtags?

Post Company Status Updates   Y/N/P

If yes, what did you write about?

Any other observations, quick wins or comments:

_____
_____
_____
_____

GOLDEN FIVE LINKEDIN ACTIVITY   Date:

Check profile visits and engage with people   Y/N/P

Observations:

Post status updates   Y/N/P

If yes, what did you write about?

Comment on other people's content   Y/N/P

Observations:

Comment on content around followed hashtags   Y/N/P

Which hashtags?

Post Company Status Updates   Y/N/P

If yes, what did you write about?

Any other observations, quick wins or comments:

_____
_____
_____
_____

GOLDEN FIVE LINKEDIN ACTIVITY   Date:

Check profile visits and engage with people   Y/N/P

Observations:

Post status updates   Y/N/P

If yes, what did you write about?

Comment on other people's content   Y/N/P

Observations:

Comment on content around followed hashtags   Y/N/P

Which hashtags?

Post Company Status Updates   Y/N/P

If yes, what did you write about?

Any other observations, quick wins or comments:

_____
_____
_____
_____

GOLDEN FIVE LINKEDIN ACTIVITY   Date:

Check profile visits and engage with people   Y/N/P

Observations:

Post status updates   Y/N/P

If yes, what did you write about?

Comment on other people's content   Y/N/P

Observations:

Comment on content around followed hashtags   Y/N/P

Which hashtags?

Post Company Status Updates   Y/N/P

If yes, what did you write about?

Any other observations, quick wins or comments:

_____
_____
_____
_____

GOLDEN FIVE LINKEDIN ACTIVITY   **Date:**

Check profile visits and engage with people   Y/N/P

Observations:

Post status updates   Y/N/P

If yes, what did you write about?

Comment on other people's content   Y/N/P

Observations:

Comment on content around followed hashtags   Y/N/P

Which hashtags?

Post Company Status Updates   Y/N/P

If yes, what did you write about?

Any other observations, quick wins or comments:

_____
_____
_____
_____

If you would like further copies of this planner, please contact us and we will send you a file with more pages.

And if you have found the book useful, please consider giving it a five-star review because this helps to keep it visible on Amazon. Thank you.

About the Author

Philip Calvert is a specialist in helping financial advisers to leverage online professional networking as part of their sales, marketing and communication strategies.

Philip is in demand as a LinkedIn expert and speaks at conferences and events worldwide. Clients who Philip has worked with include University of Cambridge, Santander, Scottish Widows, Standard Life, Maserati, Canon, Fiat, Pfizer and multiple financial advice firms. He is a Fellow of the UK Professional Speaking Association.

To book Philip to speak at your event, contact him at philip@philipcalvert.com or through LinkedIn.

Other Books for Financial Advisers by Philip Calvert

All of the following are available on Amazon:

Marketing for Financial Advice Professionals: Proven Tips and Techniques to Attract More of your Dream Clients in the Digital Age

Successful Seminar Selling for Financial Advisers: The Financial Planner's Guide to Attracting Profitable New Leads through Seminars, Workshops & Client Events

Social Media Strategy Planner for Financial Advisers, IFAs, Wealth Managers and Financial Planners

56 New Income Streams for Financial Advisers: How to Turn your Financial Planning Expertise & Experience into Profitable Information Products for the Digital Age

The Financial Planner's Daily Journal: Helping Financial Advisers to Achieve their Goals through Daily Journaling

Disclaimer and Terms of Use

This book is provided for research and educational purposes. You do not have resell rights or giveaway rights to any portion of this publication. No part of this publication may be transmitted or reproduced in any way without the prior written permission of the author. Violations of this copyright will be enforced in law.

The information services and resources provided in this book are based upon the current LinkedIn platform and internet marketing environment. The techniques presented have been extraordinarily lucrative and rewarding to LinkedIn users and internet marketers worldwide, however because LinkedIn and the internet are constantly changing, the sites and services presented in this book may change, cease or expand with time.

We hope that the skills and knowledge acquired from this book will provide you with the ability to adapt to inevitable internet evolution. However, we cannot be held responsible for changes that may affect the applicability or effectiveness of these techniques.

Any earnings or other results quoted, are based on our own and the testing of other marketers and are estimates of what we believe you could earn. There is no assurance you will do as well as stated in any examples and could be influenced by a variety of factors, not least of which include site functionality, work ethic and market conditions. If you rely upon any figures provided, you must accept the entire risk of not doing as well as the information provided.

All product names, logos and artwork mentioned in this book are copyrights of their respective owners. None of the owners have sponsored or endorsed this publication.

Philip Calvert is neither employed by or affiliated to LinkedIn Corporation in any way and is the author or this book as an independent marketing consultant and speaker.

While all attempts have been made to verify information provided, the author assumes no responsibility for errors, omissions or contrary interpretation on the subject matter herein. LinkedIn Corporation also reserves the right to alter or remove features mentioned within this book at any time. Any perceived slights of people or organisations are unintentional. The purchaser or reader of this publication assumes responsibility for the use of these materials and information.

No guarantees of income are made. The author reserves the right to make changes and assumes no responsibility or liability whatsoever on behalf of any purchaser or reader of these materials.

The purchaser and reader assume full responsibility for compliance and compliant use of the material in this book, as defined by their respective regulatory body if applicable. No guarantees are made by the author that any of the ideas presented in this book will be acceptable under the purchaser or reader's local compliance regime.

Copyright© Philip Calvert 2020. All Rights Reserved

www.ingramcontent.com/pod-product-compliance
Lightning Source LLC
Chambersburg PA
CBHW071354210526
45465CB00001B/91